CHUANG TZU'S
NEI P'IEN

Psychotherapeutic
Commentaries

Book Cover Symbolism
Cinnabar Red • Spiritual Alchemy
Gold • Solar/Fire/Transforming Energy

By The Author

LAO TZU'S *TAO TE CHING*
Psychotherapeutic Commentaries
A Wayfaring Counselor'a Rendering
of the Tao Virtuosity Experience
[Regent Press, 2016]

LIEH TZU'S *HSING SHIH SHENG*
Psychotherapeutic Commentaries
A Wayfaring Counselor's Rendering
of The Nature of Real Living
[Regent Press, 2017]

LAO TZU'S *TAO TE CHING*
Soul Journeying Commentaries
A Sojourning Pilgrim's Rendering
of 81 Spirit Soul Passages
[Regent Press, 2018]

CHUANG TZU'S
NEI P'IEN
Psychotherapeutic Commentaries

A Wayfaring Counselor's Rendering

of

The Seven Interior Records

Raymond Bart Vespe

REGENT PRESS
Berkeley, California

Copyright © 2017 by Ray Vespe

Paperback
ISBN 13: 978-1-58790-378-6
ISBN 10: 1-58790-378-4

E-book
ISBN 13: 978-1-58790-379-3
ISBN 10: 1-58790-379-2

Library of Congress Control Number: 2016963479

Manufactured in the United States of America

REGENT PRESS
www.regentpress.net
regentpress@mindspring.com

Contents

Dedication . . . xi
Acknowledgements . . . xi
Characters / Chuang / Chou / Tzu . . . 1
Prologue . . . 3
Characters / Nei / P'ien / Interior Records . . . 7

Introduction . . . 9
   Authorship . . . 9
   Text . . . 9
   Language . . . 11
   Interior Records . . . 12
   Experiential Concepts . . . 12
   Central Themes . . . 16
   Meditative Practices . . . 18
   Wu States . . . 20
   Yu States . . . 22
   Meditative Practices/Phenomenology . . . 24
   Meditative Practices/Wu-States/Yu-States . . . 25
   Taoist Knowing/Having/Doing/Being . . . 28
   Table One . . . 30
   Metaphors . . . 35
   Commentaries . . . 36
   On Attending . . . 37
   Rendition . . . 39

Characters / Hsin Chai / Heart-Mind Fasting . . . 45
   Record One / Hsiao Yao Yu /
   Carefree Wandering in Vastness . . . 47
      Central Themes . . . 49
      Text and Commentaries
         1. Vast and Tiny . . . 50
         2. Long-Lived and Short-Lived . . . 51

3. Great and Small . . . 52
4. Superfluous and Economical . . . 53
5. Limited and Unlimited . . . 54
6. Irrelevant and Relevant . . . 55
7. Huge and Useful . . . 56
8. Big and Useless . . . 57

CHARACTERS / TSO WANG / SITTING FORGETTING . . . 59
  RECORD TWO / CH'I WU LUN /
  EQUALIZING MATTERS DISCOURSING . . . 61
    CENTRAL THEMES . . . 63
    TEXT AND COMMENTARIES
      1. The Music of Heaven . . . 65
      2. Broad and Narrow . . . 66
      3. One and Many . . . 67
      4. Living and Dying . . . 68
      5. Right and Wrong . . . 69
      6. Absolute and Relative . . . 70
      7. This and That . . . 71
      8. Acceptable and Unacceptable . . . 72
      9. Three in the Morning . . . 73
      10. Loss and Completion . . . 74
      11. Something and Nothing . . . 76
      12. Unity and Multiplicity . . . 77
      13. Discriminating and Embracing . . . 78
      14. Heaven and Earth . . . 79
      15. Wording and Not-Wording . . . 79
      16. Trying and Letting-Go . . . 80
      17. Knowing and Not-Knowing . . . 81
      18. Dreaming and Awakening . . . 82
      19. Winning and Losing . . . 84
      20. Light and Shadow . . . 85
      21. Chuang Tzu and a Butterfly . . . 86

CHARACTERS / YUAN YU / ORIGIN WANDERING ... 89
  RECORD THREE / YANG SHENG CHU /
  NOURISHING LIFE'S HOST ... 91
    CENTRAL THEMES ... 93
    TEXT AND COMMENTARIES
      1. Following the Middle Way ... 94
      2. Frictionless Activity ... 95
      3. Heaven-Given Spirit ... 96
      4. Not Hiding from Heavenly Tao ... 97

CHARACTERS / TAO CHU / CHU / CH'U / TAO RESIDING ... 99
  RECORD FOUR / JEN CHIEN SHIH /
  BEING HUMAN AMID WORLDLY AFFAIRS ... 101
    CENTRAL THEMES ... 103
    TEXT AND COMMENTARIES
      1. Internalizing Tao ... 105
      2. Virtuosity and Fame ... 106
      3. Plans and Strategies ... 107
      4. Heart-Mind Fasting ... 108
      5. Fate and Duty ... 110
      6. Words and Trust ... 111
      7. Following and Harmonizing ... 113
      8. Usefulness of Uselessness - 1 ... 114
      9. Usefulness of Uselessness - 2 ... 116
      10. Usefulness of Uselessness - 3 ... 117
      11. Usefulness of Uselessness - 4 ... 118

CHARACTERS / HSING / INBORN NATURE / HUA /
TRANSFORMING ... 121
  RECORD FIVE / TE CH'UNG FU /
  VIRTUOSITY FULFILLING AGREEMENT ... 123
    CENTRAL THEMES ... 125
    TEXT AND COMMENTARIES
      1. Constancy and Unity ... 126
      2. Destiny and Virtuosity ... 128
      3. Virtuosity and Heaven - 1 ... 129

  4. Virtuosity and Spirit - 1 . . . 130
  5. Virtuosity and Wholeness . . . 132
  6. Virtuosity and Formlessness . . . 133
  7. Virtuosity and Forgetting . . . 134
  8. Virtuosity and Heaven - 2 . . . 135
  9. Virtuosity and Spirit - 2 . . . 136

CHARACTERS / CHEN / TRUE / JEN / HUMAN BEING . . . 139
 RECORD SIX / TA TSUNG SHIH /
 GREAT KINDRED TEACHER . . . 141
  CENTRAL THEMES . . . 143
  TEXT AND COMMENTARIES
   1. True Human Being . . . 145
   2. Breath and Life . . . 146
   3. Self and Others . . . 147
   4. Integrity and Light . . . 148
   5. Heaven's Tao . . . 149
   6. Earth's Tao . . . 150
   7. Manifestations of Tao . . . 151
   8. Transmitting Tao . . . 152
   9. Transforming in Tao - 1 . . . 154
   10. Transforming in Tao - 2 . . . 155
   11. Forgetting in Tao . . . 156
   12. Simplifying and Forgetting . . . 158
   13. Forgetting and Wandering . . . 159
   14. Sitting Forgetting . . . 160
   15. Poverty and Destiny . . . 162

CHARACTERS / TZU / FREEDOM / LE / HAPPINESS . . . 163
 RECORD SEVEN / YING TI WANG /
 APPROPRIATE ATTENDING AND REGULATING . . . 165
  CENTRAL THEMES . . . 167
  TEXT AND COMMENTARIES
   1. Perfect Virtuosity . . . 168
   2. Governing with Virtuosity . . . 169
   3. Governing the World . . . 170
   4. Enlightened Governing . . . 171

5. There is More to It . . . 173
6. Guidelines for Governing . . . 175
7. Undifferentiated Being . . . 176

CHARACTERS / MING / DESTINY /CH'ENG /CH'UAN / COMPLETION . . . 179
   CONCLUSION . . . 181
      Psychotherapeutic Commentaries . . . 181
      Psychotherapy/Counseling . . . 181
      Patients/Counselees . . . 183
      Psychotherapists/Counselors . . . 185
      Practical Applications . . . 187
      Summaries . . . 187
      Synopses . . . 193
      Comparisons . . . 197
      Table Two . . . 204
      Psychopathology . . . 210

CHARACTERS / T'IEN / HEAVEN / TI / EARTH / LIEN / CONNECT . . . 215
APPENDIX ONE . . . 217
   TALES FROM THE OUTER/MISCELLANEOUS RECORDS
      RECORD 19 MASTERING LIFE
         The Cicada Catcher . . . 217
         The Ferryman . . . 218
         The Archer . . . 218
         The Rooster Trainer . . . 219
         The Swimmer . . . 220
         The Bell Stand Carver . . . 221
         Forgetting . . . 222
         Nourishing a Bird . . . 222
      RECORD 20 THE MOUNTAIN TREE
         The Empty Boat . . . 223
         The Bell Maker . . . 224
      RECORD 22 KNOWLEDGE WANDERED NORTH
         The Buckle Maker . . . 225

RECORD 24 THE RECLUSE AND THE RULER
   Dog and Horse Judging . . . 226
RECORD 26 EXTERNAL THINGS
   Forgotten Words . . . 227
RECORD 28 GIVING AWAY A THRONE
   Double Injury . . . 227
RECORD 32 LIEH TZU
   Chuang Tzu's Funeral . . . 229

APPENDIX TWO . . . 231
   Quick Reference to Interior Record Tales

APPENDIX THREE . . . 237
   Excerpts from the Outer/Miscellaneous Records

NOTES . . . 239

EPILOGUE . . . 249
   The Way of Ignoring . . . 249
   The Tao of Abstaining . . . 250
   The Way of Attaching . . . 250
   The Tao of Relinquishing . . . 250
   The Way of Erring . . . 251
   The Tao of Sourcing . . . 251
   The Way of Separating . . . 252
   The Tao of Uniting . . . 252
   The Way of Ego-Being . . . 252
   The Tao of Tao Jen . . . 253

CHARACTERS/TAO/T'UNG/IDENTITY . . . 255
CODA . . . 257
REFERENCES . . . 259
ABOUT THE AUTHOR . . . 261

Dedication

For Tao-Masters, Alan Wilson Watts, Al Chung-liang Huang and Gia-fu Feng who; in seriously and playfully embodying, personifying, living, enacting and enjoying the Reality, Truth, Beauty and Harmony of Tao; modeled for me what it is and what it means to be an awake, wise, true and free Human Being. Thank you so very very much for the inspiration you have provided me by being yourselves and by living the Spirit, Body, Heart and Soul of Tao.

Acknowledgements

Of all of the so-called psychotic, autistic, neurotic and disabled; the stigmatized, marginalized, pathologized and victimized and the odd, peculiar, strange and eccentric human beings I have had the blessing to meet during my wanderings and wonderings in my personal and professional worlds. Thank you so very very much for being and sharing yourselves and for providing me with the opportunity to allow, accept and appreciate and to deepen, enrich and fulfill the precious gift, reality and experience of being a human being in this lifetime.

Gratitude, once again, to my youngest daughter, Arianna Selene Lewin, and my son-in-law, Ashley Evan Lewin for their ongoing encouragement and support and for their assistance in making my laptop computer user friendly for word-processing the manuscript for this book and for entering it into a flash drive storage gadget.

Thanks and appreciation, once again, to Mark Weiman of Regent Press for his midwifing the gestation, timely birthing and publication of this companion book to his publication of *Lao Tzu's Tao Te Ching: Psychotherapeutic Commentaries. A Wayfaring Counselor's Rendering of the Tao Virtuosity Experience.*

CHUANG

莊

Serene
Serious/sedate/solemn
Correct in conduct
Cottage/house
Hamlet/village
Workshop

CHOU

周

Revolve/go round/encircle
Encompassing/all around
Ubiquitous/everywhere at once
Whole/complete/universal
Thorough/comprehensive
Thoughtful/assisting

TZU

子

Son/child/boy
Philosopher/Master

A serene human being/serious philosopher/ universal Master who is correctly going along/ reaching an encompassing/comprehensive perspective/stopping and thoughtfully/ usefully assisting fellow human beings.[1]

Prologue

Perhaps the best way to begin this rendition of the *Interior Records / Nei P'ien* is to identify some of the complementary characteristics of Lao Tzu and Chuang Tzu by initially excerpting two descriptions from Record 33 of *The Chuang Tzu* text and by subsequently making some comparisons gleaned from the literature of Lao Tzu's *Tao Te Ching* and Chuang Tzu's *Nei P'ien*.

Lao Tzu

Considering the Source/Tao as pure and accumulation as insufficiency and living alone and peacefully in Spiritual brightness is the ancient art of Tao. The mountain passkeeper, Yin Hsi,[2] and Lao Tzu are happily identifying *as* these realities and *as* Tao *as* the Great Unity of constant Non-Being and Being manifesting essentially *as* emptiness and non-harming and outwardly *as* softness, gentleness and humility.

Yin Hsi is saying that True human beings are not self-invested and all beings are revealing themselves to them. Their activity is water-like, their stillness is mirror-like and their responding is echo-like; they are open-minded and still-willed like clear and calm water; harmoniously identifying *as* Tao and are never going ahead of, but always following, human beings.

Lao Tzu is a True Human Being identifying *as* the feminine, deep, dark, below and behind, empty and sufficient; being a valley-like stream nourishing the world. His activity is frictionless, seamless, economical, effortless and blameless and his relationships are deep, soft, generous, allowing and harmless; his greatest achievements as a True Human Being.

Chuang Tzu

Being boundless and formless, constantly changing and transforming, joining Heaven and Earth and their Spiritual brightness, considering everything impartially and equally and fully forgetting is the ancient art of Tao.

Chuang Tzu is freely and happily presenting these realities often using odd, outlandish, bold and unbound language. He is regarding his times from a multitude of perspectives with relativity and equality and is using evocative and provocative words that are reflecting the endless changes, truths and breadth of the human world.

Chuang Tzu is coming and going alone with the pure Spirit of Heaven-Earth, is not inflated or arrogant and is living with the ordinariness of his age without judging right or wrong. Although his words are often strange, unconventional, playful and jesting; they are replete with endless relevant truths.

Chuang Tzu is wandering with both the Creator above and befriending human beings below who have transcended beginnings and endings, living and dying. His understanding of the Source/Tao is deeply penetrating, vastly expansive and freely unlimited. He is attuning to, according with and riding on ancestral Truth to great heights but also is responding to the many changes in the world of things. Chuang Tzu is setting forth perennially valid truths that cannot be denied, ignored or refuted; yet is himself being obscure and arcane, not easily comprehended or completely understood.

	Lao Tzu	**Chuang Tzu**
Identity	Legendary figure	Historical person
Dates	Spring/Autumn period c. 770-475 BCE	Warring States period c. 475-221 BCE
Place	Feudal State of Ch'u	Feudal State of Sung
Climate	Socio-political upheaval	Bloody internecine warfare
Position	Court archivist	Independent scholar
Ethos	Wise governing	Free living
Fate	Left China	Stayed in China
	Opted out	Didn't buy in
	Grieve/leave	Stay/play
Text	*Tao Te Ching*	*Nei P'ien*
	Disputed authorship	Accepted authorship
	Possible compilation	Subsequent elaboration
Structure	81 Passages	7 Records
Form	Adages/maxims	Tales/accounts
Style	Formal/declarative	Anecdotal/illustrative
	Abstract/prescriptive	Personal/descriptive
	Concise/poetic	Narrative/humorous
Focus	Advice for rulers	Examples of individuals
	Wise governing	True living
	Earth-focused wisdom	Heaven-centered freedom
	Regulating/harmony	Transforming/transcendence
	Simplicity/tranquility	Carefreeness/uselessness
	Peace/contentment	Wandering/happiness
Some Concepts	Bipolarity/complementarity	Equality/interchangeability
	Alternating/reversing	Relativity/perspective
	Circulating/returning	Inevitability/completing
Practices	Letting-be	Heart-Mind Fasting
	Letting-go	Sitting Forgetting
	Going-with	Origin Wandering
	Being-with	Tao Residing
Sage	Sheng Jen	Chen Jen
	Sacred/wise human being	True/free human being
	Listens/hears/understands	Looks/sees/questions
	Obeys/speaks/transmits	Describes/lives/forgets
	Inner Tao-nature	Inborn Tao-nature
	Efficacious power	Transformative in-fluence

	Lao Tzu	**Chuang Tzu**
Sage (cont.)	Gifts/Virtuosity Not conflict/contend Union with Constant Tao Accord with Natural Law Attune to Mystery of Tao Guiding principle of Tao Remember Tao to regulate	Arts of Tao/knack Not dispute/debate Union with Vast Tao Accord with World Process Attune to Destiny of Tao Transforming process of Tao Forget Tao to liberate
Methods	Advise/counsel re: realities Instruct the conventional Inform governing Re-empower authority Impart Earthly wisdom	Clarify/amplify re: truths Deconstruct the conventional Transform governing Disempower authority Model Heavenly freedom
Goal	Living Sacredly/wisely/ harmoniously/peacefully within limits	Living truly/freely/ equally/happily beyond bounds
Caveat	Tao when spoken is not Constant Tao. (Passage 1) Those who understand don't speak. Those who speak don't understand. (Passage 56).	Once you get meaning you can forget words. When can I meet those who have forgotten words so I can have a word with them? (Record 26).

NEI 内
Inner/inside/within
Interior/heart
Enter/into

P'IEN 篇
Article/essay
Chapter/section
Bamboo slip/tablet

Entering into the interior/heart of matters and recording experiences in writing.

INTRODUCTION

Authorship

Unlike Lao Tzu, the legendary author of the *Tao Te Ching* whose actual existence is disputed by sinologists, Chuang Tzu, also known as Chuang Chou, is generally thought to be an actual human being. He reportedly lived from c. 365-286 BCE in the feudal state of Sung (c. 1113-285 BCE) in Southern China during the Warring States/Chan Kuo period (c. 475-221 BCE) of the Later/Eastern Chou Dynasty (c. 770-221 BCE), a time of bloody internecine warfare between feudal rulers vying for hegemony. Chuang Tzu apparently once briefly held an official position before leaving it to live as an independent schlolar who eventually became a destitute recluse. He is regarded as the second most influential individual, next to Lao Tzu, in the ancient Chinese philosophical and Spiritual tradition of Taoism.

Text

Chuang Tzu is regarded as having authored the *Nan Hua Chen Ching/Southern Flowering True Scripture* which later became known as *The Chuang Tzu* in the literary tradition of naming works after their purported authors. *The Chuang Tzu* text is considered to be the second principal text of the ancient Chinese Spiritual tradition of Taoism next to the earlier classic *Tao Te Ching* attributed to the philosopher Lao Tzu.

Historical records are indicating that *The Chuang Tzu* text, dates from c. 300-250 BCE, is originally composed of fifty-two chapters which are later edited down to thirty-three and compiled sometime between c. 252-312 CE by Kuo Hsiang who also authors the first commentary on the text. This commentaried edition of *The Chuang Tzu* is the standard received text that is used for most translations.

The complete *Chuang Tzu* text of thirty-three chapters is divided into the Inner/Inside/Native/Entering Chapters/Nei P'ien (1-7), the Outer/Additional/Unofficial/Foreign Chapters/Wai P'ien (8-22) and the Miscellaneous/Heterogeneous/Mixed/Variegated Chapters/Tsa P'ien (23-33). Only the seven *Inner Chapters* are believed to be authored by Chuang Tzu, the remaining chapters being added over the years by followers and syncretists perhaps as expositions of, commentaries on or elaborations of, the original themes of the first seven *Inner Chapters*.

The characters of Chuang Tzu's stories are kings, rulers, officials, sages, philosophers, masters, teachers, shamans, disciples, students, artisans, trainers, apprentices, carpenters, butchers, cripples, amputees, hunchbacks, madmen and recluses as well as supernatural mythological beings, immortals, ancient legendary figures, fabulous animals, common creatures and even Lao Tzu, Lieh Tzu, Kung-fu Tzu/Confucius, the logician Hui Tzu and Chuang Tzu himself.

The lives and experiences of all of these beings are ultimately used to illustrate ways of being true to one's inborn Tao-nature/Te/Virtuosity; according with the particular characteristics, requirements and/or issues of one's societal position, status, occupation, activities, etc. and finding ways to live true, free and happy lives in the world and to preserve their unique individuality and Spiritual integrity, especially during times of great human tragedy and suffering.

The first seven *Inner Chapters* focus on values and themes of freedom, equality, vitality, fluidity, uselessness, integrity, Virtuosity, truth, impartiality, transformation, unity, spontaneity, self-regulation and True Human Beings/Chen Jen who are harmoniously one with transcendent Heavenly Tao above and Earthly immanent Tao below; freely and happily wandering in the Heavenly Unity of Origin and fully and enjoyably residing in and riding on the worldly multiplicity of things.

Language

The Chinese language is pictographic, rather than alphabetical. The ancient characters of seal writing, and their radicals and phonetics, directly depict the realities and identities of phenomena rather than naming them with words. The original shapes of these characters have changed throughout the years due to transcribing errors and interpolations; variations in writing instruments, mediums and styles and attempts to standardize the Chinese language. The Chinese characters also do not make grammatical distinctions regarding number, tense, voice and gender, which is challenging for making accurate translations but also is allowing for creative interpretations.

In this rendition, the personal plural pronoun 'we', the present tense and the active voice are being used without gender designation. Liberal use is being made of the gerundive, verbs used as nouns in their -ing form, and the verb 'being' preceding and modifying some nouns and verbs. Examples of the above are given as follows:

1. 'The teacher instructs the student' is being changed to 'Teacher*s are* instructing students'.
2. 'Philosophy benefits people' is being changed to 'Philosophi*zing* is benefit*ing human beings*'.
3. 'Freedom is limited by conventionality' is being changed to '*Being* free is *being* limited by *being* conventional'.
4. 'The sage is wise, he lets things be' is being changed to 'Sage*s are being* wise, *they* are lett*ing* things be'.

These grammatical changes are being made in order to provide a sense of immediacy, activity and vitality to the rendition and to avoid awkward gender distinction, alternation and/or bias.

Interior Records

In this rendition, the seven *Inner Chapters* of *The Chuang Tzu* text are titled the *Interior Records* which connotes a remembering, setting-down and documenting of the deeper and timeless heart of their teachings.

The following is a sequential listing of the titles of the seven *Interior Records* in this rendition of the *Nei P'ien*:

1. Carefree Wandering in Vastness/Hsiao Yao Yi
2. Equalizing Matters Discoursing/Ch'i Wu Lun
3. Nourishing Life's Host/Yang Sheng Chu
4. Being Human amid Worldly Affairs/Jen Chien Shih
5. Virtuosity Fulfilling Agreement/Te Ch'ung Fu
6. Great Kindred Teacher/Ta Tsung Shih
7. Appropriate Attending and Responding/Ying Ti Wang

Each of the seven *Interior Records* is being introduced by its central themes and each of the tales in each of the records is being followed by its respective psychotherapeutic commentary.

Experiential Concepts

The following experiential concepts are found throughout Lao Tzu's *Tao Te Ching* and Chuang Tzu's *Nei P'ien* and are principal ones in the Chinese Taoist philosophical/Spiritual tradition. In addition to their usual definitions, included are some of their associated meanings and characteristics, Wu/Nonbeing states, Yu/Being states and meditative practices.

Te Unique individuality/authenticity/Virtuosity.[3]
 Inborn Tao-nature/inner truth/integrity/efficacious power.
Letting-be/no 'thing'-knowing/not mental object-'contents'.
Accepting/acknowledging/appreciating/
not analyzing/not altering.

Considering/comprehending/not construing/not converting.
Respecting/receiving/not rejecting/not revising.
All-awakening/all-illuminating/all-individuating.
Sanity/sagacity/not supposing/not speculating.
Clearness/lucidity/truth/wisdom.
Heart-mind fasting.
The noetics of Tao.

Yin/ Dynamic bipolarity/interdependence/complementarity.
Yang Bipolar alternating/transforming/balancing/reverting
Ch'i to complement.
陰 Letting-go/no 'thing'-having/not emotional object-'goods'.
陽 Attuning/adjusting/according/not acquiring/not attaching.
氣 Correlating/coinciding/not coveting/not claiming.
Reflecting/releasing/not refracting/not retaining.
All-centering/all-exchanging/all-regulating.
Simplicity/sufficiency/not seeking/not seizing.
Emptiness/equality/good/harmony.
Sitting forgetting.
The dynamics of Tao.[4]

Wu Kinetic fluidity/flexibility/facility.
Wei Seamless flowing/circulating/cycling/returning to Origin.
Ch'i Going-with/no 'thing'-doing/not volitional object-'deeds'.
無 Allowing/acceding/accompanying/not asserting/
爲 not aggressing.
氣 Conforming/cooperating/not controlling/not coercing.
Responding/resonating/not resisting/not reacting.
All-yielding/all-following/all-unfolding.
Sourcing/serenity/not striving/not strategizing.
Stillness/tranquility/right/peace.
Origin wandering.
The kinetics of Tao.

Tao
道

Ultimate Reality/nonduality/ubiquity.
Inclusive joining/connecting/integrating/unifying.
Being-with/no 'thing'-being/not relational object-'others'.
Associating/affiliating/allying/not alienating/not anulling.
Co-existing/communing/not confining/not constricting.
Reuniting/residing/not restraining/not restricting.
All-encompassing/all-including/all-being.
Safety/security/not splitting/not separating.
Oneness/unity/reality/identity.
Tao residing.
The ontics of Tao.

Ch'i
氣

Energetic viability/vitality/vivacity.
Health/immunity/invulnerability/longevity.
Being-alive/no mortality.
Animating/activating.
Conserving/cultivating/not configuring/not channeling.
Revitalizing/rejuvenating/not reforming/not redirecting.
All-constituting/all-pervading/all-sustaining.
Synergy/sustainability/not scattering/not squandering.
Aliveness/viability/vitality/vivacity.
Meditative concentrating.
The energetics of Tao.[5]

Tzu Jan
自然

Natural spontaneity/ipseity/serendipity.
Of-itself-so/self-so/*as*-such/*as*-is.
Being-free/no artificiality.
Amazing/astounding.
Creating/constituting/not constructing/not composing.
Re-creating/revealing/not rehearsing/not replaying.
All-presencing/all-disclosing/all-liberating.
Spontaneity/serendipity/not staging/not simulating.
Presentness/manifesting/appearing/happening.
Meditative reflecting.
The immediacy of Tao.

Wan	Phenomenal actuality/diversity/totality.
Wu	Objective experiences/beings/things/events.
	Being-complete/no partiality.
萬	Awesome/admirable.
	Concreteness/contexture/not constructs/not contents.
物	Regarding/recognizing/not reifying/not reducing.
	All-completing/all-consummating/all-culminating.
	Specificity/splendidness/not selecting/not segregating.
	Givenness/wholeness/completeness/All This!
	Meditative contemplating.
	The immanency of Tao.

Tao	Human impartiality/universality/community.
Jen	Tao-embodied/personified/returned/identified.
	Being-Tao/no egocentricity.
道	Availability/accessibility.
	Consecrating/celebrating/not conflicting/not contending.
	Realizing/reaffirming/not rejecting/not renouncing.
人	All-embracing/all-accepting/all-abiding.
	Sacredness/Spirituality/not stereotyping/not stigmatizing.
	Humbleness/compassion/assisting/benefiting.
	Meditative absorbing.
	The ultimacy of Tao.

Central Themes

The central themes and principal experiential concepts of this rendition of the *Nei P'ien* are predominantly found in the seven *Interior Records* as follows:

RECORD ONE

Central Themes	Freedom/transcending
	Vastness/wandering
	Nonduality/uselessness
Main Concept	Tao/Ultimate Reality
Energy	Absolute Ch'i
Freedom From	Limitedness/perspective
Tale	*The Fish and the Bird*

RECORD TWO

Central Themes	Bipolarity/equality
	Oneness/interchangeability
	Reciprocating/relativity
Main Concept	Yin/Yang Ch'i Dynamics
Energy	Reversing Ch'i
Freedom From	One-sidedness/partiality
Tale	*Chuang Tzu and a Butterfly*

RECORD THREE

Central Themes	Energy/vitality
	Centrality/harmony
	Spirit/nourishing
Main Concept	Ch'i/Vital Energy
Energy	Primordial Ch'i
Freedom From	Extremes/deadness
Tale	*The Ruler's Cook*

Record Four

Central Themes	Fluidity/fasting
	Openness/uselessness
	Following/not overdoing
Main Concept	Wu Wei Ch'i Kinetics
Energy	Flowing Ch'i
Freedom From	Purposes/interfering
Tale	*The Useless Tree*

Record Five

Central Themes	Virtuosity/integrity
	Potency/efficacy
	Formlessness/wholeness
Main Concept	Te/Virtuosity
Energy	Individualizing Ch'i
Freedom From	Externals/judgments
Tale	*The Ugly Man*

Record Six

Central Themes	Trueness/impartiality
	Forgetting/identifying
	Transmission/transformation
Main Concept	Chen Jen/True Human Being
Energy	Personifying Ch'i
Freedom From	Falseness/egocentricity
Tale	*The Hunchbacked Woman*

Record Seven

Central Themes	Spontaneity/totality
	Mastery/completion
	Mirror-mind/Heart center
Main Concept	Tzu Jan/Self-So
Energy	Presencing Ch'i
Freedom From	Unnaturalness/incompleteness
Tale	*Hun Tun*

Meditative Practices

The four meditative practices found in the seven *Interior Records* are Heart-Mind Fasting/Hsin Chai, Sitting Forgetting/Tso Wang, Origin Wandering/Yuan Yu and Tao Residing/Tao Chu/C'hu. The first two practices essentially involve sensory, conceptual, emotional and volitional withdrawal, detachment, relinquishment and cessation that open the way for the sourcing, originating, enacting and actualizing of the latter two practices. The meditative practices minimize the tendencies and activities of our heart-mind to make objectified 'things', 'goods', 'deeds' and 'others' out of the natural realities of human existence, phenomena of awareness and actualities of human experience.

Heart-Mind Fasting/Hsin Chai
Abstaining/refraining from typical sensory-based input and observing/witnessing cognitive/conceptual activities of mind.
Not adding/not generating more mental 'contents'/not taking in/not making up/not construing.

Sitting Forgetting/Tso Wang
Divesting/relinquishing of typical sensory-based content and detaching/releasing affective/emotional activities of heart.
Subtracting/not retaining more emotional 'goods'/letting out/not keeping in/not retaining.

Origin Wandering/Yuan Yu
Sourcing/originating of typical motives/intentions and implementations/executions of conative/volitional activities of will.
Wandering before the beginning of volitional 'deeds'/not planning/not devising/not contriving.

Tao Residing/Tao Chu/Ch'u
Joining/integrating of typical separations/divisions and relations/associations of unitive/relational activities of being.

Abiding in the co-existing of relational 'others'/not isolating/
not alienating/not excluding.

The following are further elaborations of the four meditative practices.

Heart-Mind Fasting
Letting things/beings be.
Abstaining from the mental ignorance of knowing object-'contents'. Epistemological clearness.
No 'thing'-knowing/knowing no-'thing'/No-thing/Tao 'knowing'.
Letting things/beings exist and appear individually/truly as absolutely unique and self- empowering.
Acknowledging/accepting/appreciating/respecting/receiving beings/things as they are.
Not abstracting/altering/rejecting/revising/beings/things.
Being Te-like. Truth/Virtuosity/wisdom.

Sitting Forgetting
Letting things/beings go.
Divesting of the emotional attachment to having object-'goods'. Aesthetic emptiness.
No 'thing'-having/having no-'thing'/No-thing/Tao 'having'.
Letting things/beings alternate and transform reciprocally/harmoniously as bipolar complements and self-reversing.
Attuning to/adjusting to/according with/reflecting/relinquishing things/beings as they are.
Not acquiring of/attaching to/refracting/retaining beings/things.
Being Yin/Yang Ch'i-like. Good/beauty/harmony.

Origin Wandering
Going with things/beings.
Ceasing of the volitional error of doing object-'deeds'. Ethical stillness.
No 'thing'-doing/doing no-'thing'/No-thing/Tao 'doing'.

Letting things/beings flow and unfold effortlessly/seamlessly from original sources and self-returning.
Allowing/assisting/accompanying/responding to/replying to things/beings as they are.
Not asserting/aggressing against/resisting/reacting to things/beings.
Being Wu Wei Ch'i-like. Right/grace/peace.

Tao Residing
Being with things/beings.
Ending of the relational separation of being object-'others'. Ontological oneness.
No 'thing'-being/being no-'thing'/No-thing/Tao 'being'.
Letting things/beings unite and abide wholly/fully as wayfaring companions and self-completing.
Associating/affiliating/allying/reuniting/residing with things/beings as they are.
Not alienating/abandoning/restricting/restraining things/beings.
Being Tao-like. Reality/unity/identity.

Wu-States

The four Wu/Nonbeing states that are associated with the above four meditative practices are, respectively, Non-Knowing/Wu Chih, Non-Having/Wu Yu, Non-Doing/Wu Wei and Non-Being/Wu Yu.

Non-Knowing/Wu Chih
No 'thing'-knowing/No-'thing' knowing/without knowing a 'thing'/Tao-'knowing'.
Not cluttering mind with more thoughts/concepts/facts/data.
Not mental ignorance/knowing about/defining/naming object-'things'/'contents'.
Non objectifying/externalizing/abstracting/analyzing/interpreting/concluding.

Letting-be/leaving as is/accepting/acknowledging/appreciating/
    receiving.

Non-Having/Wu Yu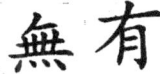

No 'thing'-having/No-'thing' having/without having a 'thing'/
    Tao-'having'.
Not littering heart with more feelings/desires/property/'stuff'.
Not emotional attachment/holding onto/owning/storing
    object-'things'/'goods'.
Non objectifying/desiring/evaluating/investing/pursuing/
    acquiring.
Letting-go/jettisoning baggage/attuning/accomodating/
    according/reflecting.

Non-Doing/Wu Wei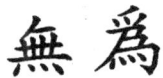

No 'thing'-doing/No-'thing' doing/without doing a 'thing'/
    Tao-'doing'.
Not busying will with more doings/makings/purposes/plans.
Not volitional error/doing of/implementing/performing
    object-'things'/'deeds'.
Non objectifying/controlling/forcing/manipulating/directing/
    interfering.
Going-with/remembering Source/allowing/agreeing/
    accompanying/responding.

Non-Being/Wu Yu

No 'thing'-being/No-'thing' being/without being a 'thing'/
    Tao-'being'.
Not separating being with more splits/divisions/dualities/
    fragments.
Not relational separation/being apart/marginalizing/distancing
    object-'things'/'others'.
Non objectifying/severing/isolating/alienating/dissociating/
    negating.

Being-with/uniting the 'ride'/affiliating/allying/abiding/
residing.

This is the meaning of Tao as nameless, empty, still and one complete whole, i.e., we are not naming/labeling, possessing/owning, causing/making and separating/dividing whatever phenomena that we are consciously aware of and experiencing into objectified 'things', e.g., mental 'contents', emotional 'goods', volitional 'deeds' and relational 'others'. Our experiencing of things and beings, then, is a No-thing or Tao-knowing, having, doing and being; a knowing-, having-, doing- and being-Tao.

Yu-States

The four meditative practices and their associated Wu/Nonbeing states open the way to their respective Yu/Being states of clearness, emptiness, stillness and oneness.

Clearness/Ming/Nao/clear mind/clarity. 明腦
Te - the epistemological ground of mental clearness.
Non naming awareness into a 'thing' to know.
Experiencing living/being without ignorance/concept/
  content-free.
Regarding/beholding/witnessing.
Appreciating the givenness of whatever phenomena are natu-
  rally presenting themselves to, and appearing in, the clear
  field/focus of conscious awareness and experience.
Openness to truth/integrity/wisdom.

Emptiness/Hsu/Hsin/empty heart/vacuity. 虛心
Yin/Yang Ch'i - the axiological center of emotional emptiness.
Non owning experience as a 'thing' to have.
Experiencing living/being without attachment/investment/

preference-free.
Releasing/abandoning/forgetting.
According with the goodness of whatever phenomena are naturally occurring in, and experienced in, the empty field/focus of conscious awareness/experience.
Openness to good/beauty/harmony.

Stillness/Ning/Chi/still will/tranquility 寧志
Wu Wei Ch'i - the ethical Source of volitional stillness.
Non manipulating activity as a 'thing' to do.
Experiencing living/being without error/motive/plan-free.
Yielding/flowing/following.
Allowing of the rightness of whatever phenomena are naturally unfolding from, and proceeding in, the still Tao-Source/Origin of conscious awareness/experience.
Openness to right/grace/peace.

Oneness/I/Tsai/whole being/unity 一在
Tao - the ontological space of relational oneness.
Non externalizing being as a 'thing' to be.
Experiencing living/being without separation/division/fragment-free.
Connecting/integrating/sharing.
Abiding with the oneness of whatever phenomena are naturally affiliated with, and joining in, the unitary field/focus of conscious awareness/experience.
Openness to reality/unity/identity.

Meditative Practices / Phenomenology

The four meditative practices of Heart-Mind Fasting, Sitting Forgetting, Origin Wandering and Tao Residing closely resemble four stages of the philosophical methodology of Western empirical/existential and transcendental/ontological phenomenlogy as follows:

Deconstituting the empirical ego and its phenomenal object-contents by:
1. Suspending presuppositions and preconceptions in order to openly witness and clearly receive the 'givenness' of the objective phenomena of lived human experience as they are presenting themselves to/in conscious awareness.
2. Bracketing out (the epoche) conceptions and definitions in order to accurately reflect and comprehensively explicate the objective phenomena of lived human experience as they are constituting themselves as subjective experiences in/of conscious awareness.

Reconstituting the Transcendental Ego and its intentional subjective-context by:
3. Reductively reaching and reflexively disclosing the implicit Transcendental Ego which originates, intends and constitutes the phenomena of lived human experience.
4. Describing the many freely varying forms and ways the phenomena of lived human experience are constituting and manifesting as the implicit Transcendental Ego.

The following table identifies the four meditative practices and their correlation with the stages of phenomenological methodology as well as several other correlations:

Heart-Mind Fasting	Sitting Forgetting	Origin Wandering	Tao Residing
Negating	Negating	Affirming	Affirming
Abstaining	Relinquishing	Sourcing	Residing
Suspending	Bracketing Out	Origin Disclosing	Freely Varying
Deconstituting	Deconstituting	Reconstituting	Reconstituting
Clearing/emptying/opening		Presencing/manifesting/appearing	
Kenosis/kenotic		Epiphany/epiphanic	
Shunyata/Emptiness/Nothing/Void		Tathata/Suchness/Everything/Plenum	
Concentration	Reflection	Contemplation	Absorption
Letting-Be	Letting-Go	Going-With	Being-With
Clearness/clarity	Emptiness/vacuity	Stillness/tranquility	Oneness/unity

The meditative practices of Heart-Mind Fasting/letting-be/clearness and Sitting Forgetting/letting-go/emptiness open the way to the meditative practices of Origin Wandering/going-with/Sourcing and Tao Residing/being-with/oneness.

Meditative Practices
Wu- States / Yu-States

It is not that as human beings we are knowing, having, doing and/or being no-thing; but that we are not objectifying what we are knowing, having, doing and being exclusively in terms of conceptualized mental 'contents', desired emotional 'goods', planned volitional 'deeds' and separated relational 'others'. This kind of no-'thing'/Wu knowing, having, doing and being is a state, condition or quality much like that of the innocent awareness, natural attachments, spontaneous activity and social identifications characteristic of young children.

This way of knowing, having, doing and being is not a mental knowing of construed, defined and named object-'contents'; an emotional having of pursued, acquired and owned object-'goods'; a volitional doing of intended, planned and executed object-'deeds' or a relational being of separated, alienated and dissociated object-'others'. Mental/cognitive awarenesses, emotional/affective possessions, volitional/conative behaviors and relational/unitive identifications are not dualistically experienced as knower-known, owner-owned, actor-action and ego-other subject-object relationships.

In early childhood, this is a natural/organic/integral state of being, but, later in life, is one that requires conscious awareness and cultivation to be in Wu-states of relative conceptlessness, desirelessness, purposelessness and relationlessness without ignorance, attachment, error and separation. Such consciousness, awareness and cultivation involve, and are greatly facilitated by, engaging in the meditative practices of heart-mind fasting, sitting forgetting, Origin wandering and Tao residing.

Heart-mind fasting is letting-be or abstaining from mentally constituting/making up the state/fact of awareness by not conceiving, construing, naming and defining abstracted and objectified 'things'/contents, i.e., knowing no-'thing', no-'thing' knowing or Tao-knowing and by acknowledging, appreciating and accepting them just *as* they are. Awareness is thus 'known'.

Sitting forgetting is letting-go or relinquishing emotionally attaching/holding onto the phenomena/events of experience by not desiring, pursuing, acquiring and owning invested and objectified 'things'/goods, i.e., having no-'thing', no-'thing' having or Tao-having by attuning to, accomodating to and according with them just *as* they are. Experiences are thus 'had'.

Origin wandering is going-with or sourcing/originating volitional activities in/as the field/space of consciousness by not intending, contriving, devising and implementing planned and objectified 'thing'/deeds. i.e., doing no-'thing', no-'thing' doing or Tao-doing by allowing, acceding to and accompanying them just *as* they are. Consciousness is thus 'done'.

Tao residing is being-with or uniting/completing relational phenomena in/as the focus/center of consciousness by not distancing, separating, dividing and fragmenting co-existing and objectified 'things'/others. i.e., being no-'thing', no-'thing' being or Tao-being by affiliating, allying and abiding with them just *as* they are. Phenomena are thus co-existent.

These four meditative practices respectively involve and result in Yu-states of clearing/ clearness of mind, emptying/emptiness of heart, stilling/stillness of will and unifying/ oneness of being and freeing/freeness of Spirit. The Yu-states are 'knowing' conceptless, pre-conceptual and pre-nominal individuality; 'having' desireless, pre-preferential and pre-possessional property, 'doing' will-less pre-purposeful and pre-operational activity; and 'being' egoless, pre-separational and pre-divisional affinity.

As such, they are the ground of clarity, the center of vacuity, the flow of tranquility and the space of unity and liberty that are pre-conditions for opening the way to receiving, reflecting, responding to and residing with just what is presencing, manifesting, unfolding and completing itself just *as* it is being/doing so in the here-now moments of conscious awareness and the phenomenal field of subjective experience.

The four meditative practices; in opening the way to non-objectified knowing/letting-be, having/letting-go, doing/going-with and being/being-with; respectively further lead to and result in experiencing end-states of discerning 'truth' and uniquenesss and awakening wiseness/sageness; beholding 'good' and beauty and attaining equalness/harmoniousness; enacting 'right' and Source and achieving gracefulness/ peacefulness and uniting 'reality' and inter-being and realizing oneness/freeness. These end-states are the wisdom, harmony, peace and freedom of Tao-focused/centered, Tao-embodied/personified, Tao-realized/actualized, Tao-identified/returned and Tao-awakened/liberated human beings.

Lao Tzu's Sheng Jen/Sacred/wise human beings and Chuang Tzu's Chen Jen/True/free human beings are such human beings who are being and living the uniquely individualized integrity, Virtuosity, potency and efficacy of their inner Tao-nature/Te; the bipolar, complementary, alternating, balancing and reversing dynamics of Yin/Yang Ch'i energy; the seamless, flowing, circulating, cycling and returning kinetics of Wu Wei Ch'i energy; the spontaneous, of-itself-so, self-like, just-so-ness and *as*-is presencing of Tzu Jan; the phenomenal variety, diversity, multiplicity, totality and richness of Wan Wu and the Ultimate Reality of transcendent Tao and the intimate actualities of immanent Tao.

Taoist Knowing/Having/Doing/Being

The following are characteristics, qualities, relationships, activities and practices of Taoist-oriented knowing, having, doing and being.

TAOIST KNOWING is a radical epistemology/logic of non-'knowing'/non-'reasoning' 'things':
1. an abstained mental 'knowing' of abstracted/construed/defined/named object-'contents'.
2. a letting-be/heart-mind fasting/refraining/restraining clearing of the cognitive ego-mind.
3. a letting-be/receiving of the uniquely materializing/individualizing forms (Te) of Tao.
4. a non-'knowing' of no 'thing'-knowing / knowing no-'thing' / thinking no 'content' or 'concept'.
5. a No-thing knowing/Tao-revealing, acknowledging and appreciating of the unique phenomena manifesting, presencing and appearing within conscious awareness and *as* human experience.

TAOIST HAVING is a radical aesthetics/axiology of non-'having'/non-'valuing' 'things':
1. a relinquished emotional 'having' of desired/invested/acquired/attached object-'goods'.
2. a letting-go/sitting forgetting/divesting/detaching/emptying of the affective ego-heart.
3. a letting-go/releasing of the dynamically alternating/reversing forms (Yin/Yang Ch'i) of Tao.
4. a non-'having' of no 'thing'-having/having no-'thing'/owning no 'good' or 'article'.

5. a No-thing having / Tao-reciprocating, attuning and according of the bipolar phenomena obtained, contained and retained within conscious awareness and *as* human experience.

TAOIST DOING is a radical ethics/politics of non-'doing'/non-'governing' 'things':
1. a restrained volitional 'doing' of motivated/planned/devised/contrived object-'deeds'.
2. a going-with/Origin wandering/yielding/following/stilling of the conative ego-will.
3. a going-with/responding to the kinetically flowing/returning forms (Wu Wei Ch'i) of Tao.
4. a non-'doing' of no 'thing'-doing/doing no-'thing'/performing no 'deed' or 'act'.
5. a No-thing doing/Tao-sourcing, allowing and accompanying of the ongoing activities unfolding, occurring and proceeding within conscious awareness and *a*s human experiencing.

TAOIST BEING is a radical ontology/metaphysics of non-'being'/non-'transcending' 'things':
1. an integrated relational 'being' of separated/isolated/alienated/dissociated object-'others'.
2. a being-with/Tao residing/communing/identifying/uniting of the disunitive ego-self.
3. a being-with/relating with the intimately joining/interconnecting forms (Tao) of Tao.
4. a non-'being' of no 'thing'-being/being no-'thing'/positing no 'other' or 'ego'.
5. a No-thing being/Tao-uniting, affiliating and abiding of the co-existing interactions of interbeing, intersubjectivity and interrelationship within conscious awareness and *as* human experiencing.

TABLE ONE

The following table depicts the four principal experiential concepts of Te, Yin/Yang Ch'i, Wu Wei Ch'i and Tao and their respective existential domains, meditative practices, Wu-states, Yu-states, openness to what is, phenomenological qualities, end-states and presence as Tao Jen, Tao-like human beings.

Experiential Concepts	TE Unique individuality	YIN/YANG CH'I Alternating energy
Existential Domains	Mental Cognitive Thinking Knowing Comprehending Understanding Structuring Constituting	Emotional Affective Feeling Having Attaining Interchanging Correlating Interacting
Meditative Practices	Heart-Mind Fasting Letting-Be Abstaining from mental object-contents Conceptless No object-ivity	Sitting Forgetting Letting-Go Relinquishing of emotional object-goods Desireless No object-ions
Wu-States Negatives	Mentally knowing no-'thing' No/not-/non- abstracting conceiving construing naming	Emotionally having no-'thing' No/not-/non- desiring seeking pursuing acquiring

	defining	owning
	classifying	claiming
	categorizing	displaying
	No knower-known	No owner-owned
Yu-States *Positives*	Acknowledging Accepting Appreciating of what is so Innocent awareness Pre-conceptual/ pre-nominal individuality Epistemological/ noetic groundedness of mental mind-body Clearness/ clarity	Attuning Adjusting According of what is so Natural appropriating Pre-preferential/ pre-possessional property Axiological/ dynamic centeredness of emotional heart-body Emptiness/ vacuity
Openness *To What Is*	Receiving/ not rejecting what is presencing in awareness just *as* it is	Reflecting/ not retaining what is manifesting as experience just *as* it is
Phenomenological *Qualities*	Te-like Uniqueness Individuality Interiority Integrity Potency Efficacy	Yin/Yang Ch'i-like Bipolarity Complementarity Alternating Reciprocating Balancing Centering

	Virtuosity	Voiding
	Genius	Reversing
End-States	Letting-Be	Letting-Go
	Discerning truth	Beholding good
	Wiseness/sageness	Equalness/harmoniousness
	Wisdom/Light	Harmony/Love
Tao Jen	Tao-awakened	Tao-centered
	Tao-realized	Tao-regulated
	Tao-embodied	Tao-attained
Experiential Concepts	Wu Wei Ch'i Circulating energy	Tao Ultimate Reality
Existential Domains	Volitional	Relational
	Conative	Unitive
	Behaving	Existing
	Doing	Being
	Enacting	Integrating
	Functioning	Uniting
	Operating	Completing
	Accomplishing	Liberating
Meditative Practices	Origin	Tao
	Wandering	Residing
	Going-With	Being-With
	Sourcing of volitional object-deeds	Joining of relational object-others
	Purposeless	Egoless
	No object-ives	No object-ifications

Wu-States *Negatives*	Volitionally doing no-'thing' No/not-/non-intending contriving devising planning implementing executing performing No actor-acted	Relationally being no-'thing' No/not-/non-distancing separating dividing fragmenting alienating isolating excluding No ego-other
Yu-States *Positives*	Allowing Acceding Accompanying of what is so Spontaneous activity Pre-purposeful/pre-operational activity Ethical/kinetic flowingness of volitional will-body Stillness/tranquility	Affiliating Allying Abiding with what is so Social identification Pre-separational/pre-divisional affinity Ontological/ontic spaciousness of relational Spirit-body Oneness/liberty
Openness *To What Is*	Responding to/not reacting to what is unfolding from consciousness just *as* it is	Residing/not restricting what is completing as phenomenon just *as* it is

Phenomenological Qualities	Wu Wei Ch'i-like Flexibility Fluidity Facility Frictionlessness Seamlessness Circulating Cycling Returning	Tao-like Ubiquity Universality Unity Identity Spontaneity Phenomenality Intimacy Ultimacy
End-States	Going-With Enacting right Gracefulness/ peacefulness Peace/Law	Being-With Uniting real Oneness/ freeness Freedom/Life
Tao Jen	Tao-sourced Tao-enacted Tao-actualized	Tao-identified Tao-returned Tao-completed

Metaphors

As in the rendition of Lao Tzu's *Tao Te Ching*, although not explicitly and specifically considered in this rendition, material in the text of Chuang Tzu's *Nei P'ien* can be understood metaphorically and identified with/*as* in the following ways:

Creator/Creatrix — *our Original nature.*
Heaven/Earth — *our celestial/terrestrial nature.*
Universe/Cosmos — *our universal nature.*
Mountains/Lakes/Trees/Et Al — *our natural nature.*
Divine/Immortal Beings — *our superhuman nature.*
Ancient/Mythological Beings — *our archetypal nature.*
Ancient/Legendary Beings — *our historical nature.*
Animals/Creatures — *our instinctual nature.*
True/Perfect Human Beings — *our Tao-nature.*
Holy/Saintly Beings — *our Sacred nature.*
Sages/Wise Human Beings — *our awakened nature.*
Masters/Teachers — *our developed nature.*
Disciples/Students — *our developing nature.*
Rulers/Leaders — *our regulating nature.*
Logicians/Philosophers — *our rational nature.*
Artisans/Trainers — *our skilled nature.*
Recluses/Hermits — *our nonconventional nature.*
Cripples/Amputees — *our virtuous nature.*
Body/Mind — *our physical/mental nature.*
Heart/Center — *our existential nature.*
Clearness/Clarity — *our conceptual nature.*
Emptiness/Vacuity — *our emotional nature.*
Stillness/Tranquility — *our volitional nature.*
Oneness/Unity — *our relational nature.*
Illness/Dying — *our mortal nature*
Destiny/Fate — *our inevitable nature*
Wholeness/Completeness — *our final nature.*
Spirit/Soul — *our Essential nature.*

Commentaries

The *Chuang Tzu* text has been commentaried upon for over one thousand seven hundred years from various perspectives, e.g., political, martial, alchemical, mystical, esoteric, yogic, religious, philosophical, etc.. The present commentary is being made from the perspective of the professional practice of psychotherapy/counseling.

Psychotherapeutic commentaries are being given for each one of the tales in each of the seven *Interior Records*. The commentaries are describing the characteristics, understandings, experiences and activities of true attending psychotherapists/counselors in the conducting of the attending psychotherapy/counseling relationship/process.

In psychotherapeutic commentaries on the *Tao Te Ching*, psychotherapists/counselors are being described as 'wise attenders' and in the *Nei P'ien*, psychotherapists/counselors are being described as 'true attenders' in keeping with respective textual distinctions between Sacred/wise human beings/Sheng Jen and true/free human beings/Chen Jen. Psychotherapy/counseling is considered as the 'attending relationship/process'.

Psychotherapy is being considered etymologically as the Greek 'psyche-therapeuein' or 'attending the Soul' which is identical to nourishing and cultivating Virtuosity/Te as our innermost, deepest, centermost, truest and utmost Tao-nature throughout our wayfaring from the originating of Tao in human birthing, through the human living of the '10,000 things' within human existing and experiencing to the returning to Tao in human dying.

True attending psychotherapy/counseling is being identified as a way of encouraging, supporting, assisting, facilitating, guiding and completing the psychological dimensions of the life-long journeying of our Human Soul as an embodied Spirit and inSpirited body. In the wayfaring journeying of our Human Soul, Tao/Ultimate Reality is considered to be identical with Spirit and Te/Virtuosity is considered to be identical with our Human Soul.[6]

Each commentary can be a rich source of, and re-source for, deep intrapsychic and interpersonal awakening, experiencing and transforming. The essential realities and meanings of the commentaries can be internlized and assimilated when read with deep and full breathing and openly and slowly in calm meditative states of concentration, reflection, contemplation and absorption, i.e., in meditative focus, openness, awareness and identification.

On Attending

In the commentaries of this rendition, as noted above, instead of being named psychotherapists/counselors, the human beings engaged in the practice of psychotherapy/ counseling are designated as 'true attenders' and psychotherapy/counseling is designated as the 'attending relationship/process'. This is consistent with the etymological meaning of psychotherapy as 'Soul' (Greek -psyche) 'attending' (Greek - therapeuein) and also is identical with Chen Jen/True human beings nourishing, cultivating and sustaining Tao as our innermost, deepest, centermost, truest and utmost nature, i.e., Te/Virtuosity.

Attending is a fundamental quality and essential factor in the psychotherapy/counseling relationship/process.[7] Also, various forms and meanings of 'attending' denote states and activities of being and consciousness that apply to four principal experiential concepts identified in this rendition, integrating them and psychotherapy/counseling practice in the following ways:

TE ❖ in the letting-be/'knowing' mode of no-'thing' knowing about, or the construing of, mental object-'contents'.

— paying attention to/mindfully, availably and receptively observing/giving focused heed to the phenomena of/in conscious awareness.

YIN/YANG CH'I ❖ in the letting-go/'having' mode of no-'thing' having of, or the attaching to, emotional object-'goods'.

— being attentive to/thoughtfully, sympathetically and kindly considering/caring about/empathizing with the needs/comfort of others.

WU WEI CH'I ❖ in the going-with/'doing' mode of no-'thing' doing of, or the performing of, volitional object-'deeds'.
 — attending to/responsively, cooperatively and appropriately taking care of necessities requiring completing.

TAO ❖ in the being-with/'being' mode of no-'thing' being of, or the separating of, relational object-'others'.
 — being an attender or an attendant present at/collectively joining/participating in a given place/occasion/event or looking after/staying with another as a companion/friend/professional or being concomitant to/associated with/resultant of circumstances.

Also, the various meanings of 'tending' have to do with awaiting, standing by, listening, watching over, caring for, serving, cultivating and fostering.[8]

True psychotherapists/counselors are human beings who are paying attention, being attentive and attending to as an attender present at, ready to serve and participating in the attending relationship/process and the attendant phenomena concomitantly associated with and accompanying it.

Ideally, these ways of true attending in psychotherapy/counseling involve the mental clearness, emotional emptiness, volitional stillness and relational oneness of psychotherapists/counselors and the human beings with whom they are working. These ways of attending can open the Way to co-creating and co-experiencing the unique individuality, equal reciprocity, appropriate activity and intimate intersubjectivity of the psychotherapy/counseling attending relationship/process; such that essential/necessary/appropriate actions and interactions naturally flow and organically follow from the clear and open awarenesses of, and the deep and full connections between, attending psychotherapists/counselors and human beings.

So, the healing and transforming potency, efficacy and intimacy of these ways of conducting the attending relationship/process are not only, or not so much, a matter of true attenders knowing psychological theories and concepts, making clinical assessments and judgments, implementing treatment plans and intervention strategies and utilizing psychotherapy techniques and methods as they are a function of the Spirit in which they are brought into it; the ways of being that they are bringing to it and the openness, clearness, deepness, fullness and connectedness of their presentness in it and their attentiveness to it.

True and free human living are the attentive experiencing of self-awakening, transforming and developing that are equivalent to the journeying of our Human Souls from ego-identifying with body, mind, others and the world to Self-identifying with Spirit, Psyche/Consciousness, fellow Human Beings and the Multiverse; the wayfaring from the '10,000 things' to Tao. The attending relationship/process of psychotherapy/counseling is one beneficial way of attending to, encouraging, supporting, assisting, facilitating and guiding at least some part of the natural unfolding of the wayfaring journey returning us Home to our Selves, Souls and Spirit.[8]

Rendition

In this rendition of the seven *Interior Records,* the following literary freedoms are being exercised to facilitate the reading of the tales and the making of generalizations and applications:

1. Chinese names are being eliminated and the characters in tales are variously referred to by way of their identities, positions, roles, characteristics and appearances, e.g., human beings, people, wayfarers, masters, teachers, disciples, students, sages, madmen, hermits, hunchbacks, cripples, amputees, etc..
2. Kings, princes, lords, barons and dukes are generally

referred to as rulers and leaders.
3. Sages are variously referred to as sages, Tao-Masters and wise, true and/or free human beings.
4. The names of traditional Taoist philosophers are retained, i.e., Chuang Tzu, Lao Tzu and Lieh Tzu, as well as Kung Fu Tzu/Confucius and Hui Shih Tzu, the logician.

This book, like its companion book, *Lao Tzu's Tao Te Ching: Psychotherapeutic Commentaries. A Wayfaring Counselor's Rendering of the Tao Virtuosity Experience,* is technically not a translation but, rather, a rendition and the literary equivalent of a jazz rendition characterized by occasional improvised solo departures from an original composition.

This rendition is based upon reading, studying, cross-referencing, correlating and meditating on over twenty-five English language translations, versions, interpretations, renditions, adaptations, selections and abridgements of the seven *Inner Chapters/Nei P'ien* of *The Chuang Tzu* text as well as one bilingual translation of the complete text. The central themes and commentaries of the rendition are based upon: 1) studying numerous writings in the Spiritual literature of Chinese Taoist Philosophy/ Tao Chia and Religion/Tao Chiao; 2) consulting Chinese language dictionaries and reference materials for the etymological definitions and extended meanings of many of the Chinese characters; 3) workshop experiences with several Tao-Masters and 4) teaching, training, supervising, mentoring and practicing in the field of psychotherapy in a wide variety of academic institutions, inpatient and outpatient clinical treatment facilities and centers and group and individual private practice settings during the past fifty-seven years.

This work, like its previous one on Lao Tzu's *Tao Te Ching,* is not intended to be about Chinese Taoism as yet another '-ism/-ology', 'school' or way of psychotherapy involving particular theoretical concepts and methodological techniques for use in treating specific clinical conditions or patient populations but, rather is, at the very most, a westernized urban neo-Taoist way of truly understanding and freely conducting any psychotherapy/counseling relationship/process that integrates Eastern psychospiritual and Western psychotherapeutic personal and transpersonal attitudes and approaches, regardless of particular theoretical orientations or methodological applications.

Also, this rendition is not an owner's operational/'how to do' manual for psychotherapy practice since, in general, it does not include concrete and detailed examples of specific interpretations, interactions and interventions in the attending relationship/process. The greatest emphasis of psychotherapeutic agency, potency, efficacy and intimacy is upon the natural, integral and practical modes, states and qualities of the Tao-identified being, awakened consciousness, clear awareness, full attention and deep connection of true attenders rather than upon any particular kinds of theoretical conceptions entertained, interpersonal relationships engaged in or methodological procedures utilized, e.g.,

TE/VIRTUOSITY

- mode of attending/attention *to*/heeding *of* phenomena.
- state of nondual awakeness/awareness/accepting/acknowledging.
- state of letting-be/individuality/uniqueness/integrity/receiving.
- mode of 'knowing'/clearness/consciousness/openness of mind.
- qualities of non-externalizing/abstracting/objectifying.
- qualities of non-presupposing/preconceiving/predefining.
- qualities of non-portending/interrogating/interdicting/interjecting.
- quality of intersubjective interpreting/interpretations.

YIN/YANG CH'I

- mode of attending/attentive *to*/caring *for* needs.
- state of empathic attuning/adjusting/aligning/according.
- state of letting-go/alternating/balancing/voiding/reversing.

- mode of 'having'/emptiness/centeredness/equalness of heart.
- qualities of non-assessing/evaluating/desiring.
- qualities of non-prejudging/preferring/pre-empting.
- qualities of non-extending/interpolating/interposing/interceding.
- quality of interdependent interchanging/interchanges.

Wu Wei Ch'i

- mode of attending/attending *to*/taking care *of* business.
- state of synergic entraining/acceding/allowing/accompanying.
- state of going-with/Sourcing/yielding/following/returning.
- mode of 'doing'/stillness/cooperativeness/calmness of will.
- qualities of non-controlling/manipulating/forcing.
- qualities of non-preplanning/predetermining/prefabricating.
- qualities of non-intending/interfering/interrupting/intercepting.
- quality of interactive intervening/interventions.

Tao/Ultimacy

- mode of attending/attendance *at*/participating *in* events.
- state of co-existing beingness/affiliating/allying/abiding.
- state of being-with/joining/communing/uniting/residing.
- mode of 'being'/oneness/connectedness/wholeness of being.
- qualities of non-separating/alienating/fragmenting.
- qualities of non-precedence/pre-eminence/precluding.
- qualities of non-pretending/intermixing/interlocking/interfusing.
- quality of interrelated interconnecting/interconnections.

Rather, this rendition and commentaries are, purely and simply, an opportunity to express some of whatever observations, discoveries and connections have been made during sixty-two years of integrating the psychospiritual and psychotherapeutic attitudes and approaches of the disciplines of ancient Chinese Taoism and modern Western Psychology.

The tales and commentaries of the rendition are best read in a state of quiet relaxation and open awareness, i.e., with a relatively clear mind, empty heart, still will and free Spirit, so as to allow their meanings to resonate more deeply and fully in your unique inner being and for your individual journeying and intimate wayfaring along the wilderness pathways, flowing watercourses and awaiting frontiers of Tao.

Once again, as with the rendering of, and psychotherapeutic commentary on, the *Tao Te Ching/Tao Virtuosity Experience* text; if you find this material to be of some, or any, interest, value, encouragement, support, assistance, guidance, use and/or benefit to you in awakening, discovering, experiencing, understanding and sharing your precious human being, conscious human living and unique wayfaring journeying; I am infinitely pleased and eternally grateful.

Raymond Bart Vespe
Santa Rosa, California
Summer Solstice, 2016

HSIN	CHAI/CH'I

Heart-mind	Fast/abstain
Center/midpoint/core	Purify/refine
Feeling/thinking	Open to receive
Intentions/motives	Retired/studious

Opening the way to experiencing the consistent blessings of Absolute/Heavenly Tao by:

Purifying and clearing the heart-mind of mental object-'contents'.
Abstaining from mentally/cognitively abstracting, objectifying, construing, defining, labeling, classifying and categorizing experiential phenomena.
Stepping back and letting experiential phenomena be just *as* they are presenting themselves in conscious awareness without altering, revising and converting them.
Equally respecting, regarding, witnessing, beholding, appreciating, welcoming, receiving and accepting experiential phenomena just *as* they are presencing themselves in conscious awareness.

RECORD ONE
Carefree Wandering in Vastness

HSIAO

Ramble/roam
Saunter/wander

YAO

Distant/remote
Far off/vast

YU

Swim/float
Travel/wander
Saunter/stroll
Ramble/roam

RECORD ONE

Carefree Wandering in Vastness

Central Themes

The first Record of the *Nei P'ien* is about vastness, transcendence, freedom, nonduality, wandering and uselessness.

Nature's six month alternation at the solstices is portrayed as the transforming of a Great Yin fish of the fathomless depths of Northern Earthly waters into a Great Yang bird of the limitless heights of Southern Heavenly skies. A transcendent and an immanent realm are respectively characterized as vast, boundless, remote, broad, immense and long-lived and as limited, bounded, close, narrow, small and short-lived.

True human beings are depicted as rejecting limited relative perspectives, rational-logical thinking, conventional attitudes, subjective value judgments and habitual activities. They are not accepting public office or rulership and are not seeking name, social status, famous reputation, merit or gain.

True human beings are unconcerned with relative dualistic distinctions, e.g., success-failure, praise-blame, merit-dishonor, or with irrelevant issues, external matters and worldly affairs. They are not worried about or troubled by the limitations and entanglements of ordinary human existence and are preserving their vital energy, inner nature, simplicity and Spirit.

True human beings are open to transcendent, supramental, transpersonal and non-ordinary realities and states of consciousness and are comfortable resting, relaxing, floating and wandering; happily carefree and purposeless; free and easy; in the nothingness, emptiness, openness, spaciousness and vastness of boundless, limitless and endless space-time.

Some True human beings are independent of the physical world; have developed supernatural qualities, Virtuosity/Te and abilities; are invulnerable and immune to negative and harmful external forces and are able to positively influence human beings and world events and to order, unite, protect, benefit, sustain and transform them.

True human beings are not bound and limited by the mental clutter of discursive reasoning, rational analysis, conceptual distinctions and logical arguments. They are able to make use of superordinate realities to wander carefree, uselessly and safely in the vastness of the universe, preserving their life by avoiding being exploited or injured.

1-1 ❖ Vast and Tiny

Text

Deep in the dark Northern sea, a fish of immeasurable vastness is transforming into a bird of equally immeasurable vastness. Every six months it is migrating to the Southern sea; rising up thousands of miles, creating a whirlwind, clouding endless blue skies and churning waters for thousands of miles. Then the vast bird is transforming back into the vast fish that is making its regular six month cyclical return to the Northern sea. Only great winds and deep waters can support such huge wings and fins.

Tiny birds are looking up at the vast bird, remembering that they can barely fly up to low tree branches and wondering how the vast bird can fly so high and so far. Such is the difference between vast and tiny.

Commentary

True attenders are:

Understanding the true attending relationship/process as a transformative journey of great magnitude alternating between the deep Earthly Yin waters of the unconscious and subconscious human mind and the vast Heavenly Yang skies of the conscious and supraconscious human mind.

Understanding that the true context and connection of the attending relationship/process need to be deep and full enough to provide the structure, consciousness and vital energy to support freely and regularly journeying in the vast spaciousness and dimensionality of human existence and experience.

Experiencing that the tiny ego-mind of human beings is often wondering how such an immense transformative journey is possible, given its seeming inability to rise above and get beyond its own limitations.

1-2 ❖ Long-lived and Short-lived

Text

Hiking to nearby woods is only requiring packing food for the day. Traveling one hundred or one thousand miles is requiring packing food for weeks or months. How can the tiny birds know much about such differences between short and long journeys? Little knowing and the short-lived cannot compare with Great Understanding and the long-lived.

Daytime mushrooms are not knowing dawn and dusk and Summer insects are not knowing Spring and Autumn. They are the short-lived. But there are miraculous trees whose seasons are hundreds and thousands of years long. And there is an ancient human being venerated for having lived one thousand years. They are the long-lived with which short-lived creatures and with whom human beings sadly cannot compare. Such is the long and the short of it.

Commentary

True attenders are:

Conducting brief, short-term and problem-focused attending relationship/processes as well as longer-term depth-oriented ones that are requiring more personal and professional preparation, training, development and commitment.

Experiencing that the vastness and limitlessness of a deeper attending relationship/process journey often cannot be fathomed from the limited and narrow standpoint of the ordinary transient ego-consciousness of human beings.

Understanding that the spacious reality and totality of the true transformative attending relationship/process journey are far beyond reductive and limited knowings of psychological theories, psychopathological formulations and psychotherapy techniques that sadly cannot compare with it.

1-3 ❖ Great and Small

Text

People capable of holding one minor office, organizing one small community and serving only one country are like the little birds. Wise human beings are amused by them because they themselves clearly distinguish external and internal and are unconcerned with praise and honor or blame and disgrace. While not entangled in worldly affairs, they still are limited and incomplete.

Even though Lieh Tzu[9] is light enough to ride the wind, he still needs something by which to get around and has to come back down to earth. True human beings are able to easily ride on the flowing transforming energies of Heaven-Earth and to freely wander in the infinite vastness of the universe without depending upon anything.

True human beings are Sacred, wise, complete, free and without self, name, merit or fame.

Commentary

True attenders are:

Not limited to a few theoretical formulations, clinical issues, methodological techniques or patient/counselee populations.

Clear about the inner depth of their work, relatively

disinterested in narrow specializations and indifferent to peer evaluations but, even when transpersonally-oriented, still depend upon concepts of, vehicles for and the grounding of flights into transcendent dimensions and non-ordinary states of consciousness.

Understanding the possibility of easily riding the expansively transformative energies of, and freely wandering in the spaciously infinite vastness of, higher states of supramental consciousness without depending upon ordinary ego-mind supports.

Not needing professional ego-identity, recognition, rewards or famous reputation and are simply being and living the magnitude of their Sacredness, wisdom, integrity and freedom in their practice of the attending relationship/process.

1-4 ❖ Superfluous and Economical

Text

A ruler is wanting to cede his state to a humble recluse, saying that, 'Burning torches when the sun is shining or watering fields when the rain is falling is irrelevant and wasteful. I too am irrelevant, ruling a country that is already well-ordered. You take it over.' The recluse replies, 'If I replace you, it is for name only, the semblance of reality. A small bird resting in the forest uses only one tree branch and a small mole drinking at the river takes only one bellyfull. Forget it! I have no use for ruling a state. Even if cooks are not running their kitchens well, priests do not jump in to take over.'

Commentary

True attenders are:

Not facilitating rational insights and emotional releases for human beings who are already sufficiently conscious and expressive.

Not trying to control, direct, change, improve or usurp the

self-regulating of human beings when it already is naturally and effectively operating, supporting and serving their health, growth, development and fulfillment sufficiently well enough.

Not engaging in the attending relationship/process to inflate ego-images or gain ego-status but, rather, because it is the one vocation that simply, perfectly and appropriately accords with the absolute reality, truth and uniqueness of their innermost, deepest, centermost, truest and utmost Tao-nature or Virtuosity/Te.

1-5 ❖ Limited and Unlimited

Text

One wayfarer is telling another wayfarer about someone he overheard talking about 'strange and fantastic things, far beyond human experience.' The second wayfarer asks, 'Like what?'

The first wayfarer replies, 'Holy beings are living on a distant Sacred mountain. Their skin is snow white and smooth; they are shy and gentle as young girls; they do not eat grains but breathe wind and drink dew; they ride on clouds and dragons and wander far beyond the limits of this world. They use their Spiritual energies and powers to make beings healthy and harvests bountiful. All of this is so ridiculous. I do not believe any of it!'

The second wayfarer responds, 'So it seems to you. Blind and deaf people cannot experience beautiful colors and sounds and blindness and deafness can also limit understanding, like yours do. These Holy beings, with all of their Virtuosity, are uniting everything into One. By their very existence alone, the world is ordered but they are not concerned about ordering it. Nothing can harm them. They are not drowned in rising floods or burned by scorching fires. When great rulers could be fashioned from their dust and ashes, how could they be bothered by worldly things?'

COMMENTARY

True attenders are:

Understanding that the unlimited magnitude, freedom and power of the true attending relationship/process seem ungrounded, strange, incredible, fantastic and ridiculous to the limited ego-minds of human beings and many colleagues.

Experiencing the realities of non-ordinary states of consciousness, psychic openings, Spiritual awakenings, bodily transcendence, physical invulnerability and the transformative, integrative, healing and bounteous power of their presence alone.

Cultivating and embodying the vitalizing Spiritual energies of Tao/Ch'i; are living within but beyond the 'things' and 'others' of the ordinary human world and are protecting, nourishing, harmonizing and developing human beings without necessarily being concerned about doing so.

1-6 ❖ IRRELEVANT AND RELEVANT

TEXT

An entrepeneur is failing to sell ceremonial hats and robes to people with decorated heads and tatooed bodies because they are irrelevant and useless to them.

A wise ruler loses interest in ruling the state after visiting Spiritual beings living on a remote Sacred mountain.

COMMENTARY

True attenders are:

Not attempting to market irrelevant programs to human beings who have no need for them and are not employing a variety of irrelevant and useless techniques, exercises and processes with them.

Generally less occupied with approaches that are exclusively focused upon controlling, managing and regulating the ego-functioning of human beings.

Relatively more interested in accepting the unique realities of human beings, working within their subjective experiential frames of reference and relevantly assisting them in their Self-actualizing and Spiritual developing.

1-7 ❖ Huge and Useful

Text

Logician Hui Tzu[10] is saying to Chuang Tzu, 'The seeds I planted grew into huge gourds but they are too big to be cut into ladles or to use as containers, so I broke them up.' Chuang Tzu replies, 'You certainly are unimaginative when it comes to making use of large things.'

Chuang Tzu continues, 'There is a family expert in making a salve to prevent chapped hands as part of their silk bleaching business. A wayfarer learning of this, buys their secret formula for more money than the family makes during a year of work. The wayfarer offers the salve to a ruler for use in winter naval battles and its effectiveness in preventing the chapping of soldiers' hands enables them to win the battles. The grateful ruler then awards the wayfarer with a fief and title. In both instances, the same salve is used to prevent chapped hands but for different purposes with different results. The wayfarer obtains land and a title and the family is still bleaching silk.

Now, you had these huge gourds that you broke up thinking that they were useless as ladles or containers. Why did not you use them as boats and leisurely float around in the lake? Your mind seems cluttered with small and limited concerns.'

Commentary

True attenders are:

Not usually so analytically-oriented, atomistic-reductionistic and logic-bound that they do not imaginatively and creatively know what to do with multidimensional realities and transpersonal experiences that are presenting themselves in the attending relationship/process.

Not breaking up superordinate realities into fine analytic discriminations, minute conceptual distinctions and narrow definitions that destroy their magnitude and magnificence because they are, e.g., deemed to be epiphenomena of human consciousness, psychopathological symptoms, religious delusions or spiritual psychoses.

Making use of transcendent realities and transpersonal phenomena to richly re-member, leisurely reside in and freely and happily 'ride' Tao rather than discard them through the intellectualized concepts and theoretical formulations, discursive reasoning and syllogistic logic and limited conclusions and decisions of cluttered, unimaginative and uncreative ego-minds that can only perpetuate the status quo rather than foster innovation.

1-8 ❖ Big and Useless

Text

After recovering from the previous go-around, Hui Tzu is trying again, 'Well, I also grew this big tree but its trunk is so gnarled and knotty and its branches are so twisted and crooked that it is absolutely useless to carpenters. And your words are just as big and no one can make any use of them.'

Chuang Tzu retorts, 'Weasels crouch and hide waiting to pounce on prey and when they leap out and race around they are caught in traps. And there is the yak, big as a cloud shadowing the sky, but it does not bother itself with catching a little rat.

Now you grew this big tree and are concerned with its uselessness. Why do not you imagine that it is planted in the vast and boundless land of Nothingness and wander idly around it or lie down underneath it for a carefree rest? The big tree is useless to carpenters and their axes will never do it harm or shorten its life.'

Commentary

True attenders are:

Not finding Tao to be too big, too knotty and too convoluted of a reality to be utilized as the context, ground and center of the attending relationship/process.

Observing that their analytically-oriented colleagues are often caught in their own logical traps when it comes to trying to understand the totality of Tao and its operations or to find it to be of any use in their psychotherapy/counseling practice.

Finding the immensity of Tao extremely useful for remembering the original No-thingness of human being and for freely wandering and happily resting in its emptiness, spaciousness, vastness and wholeness which can never be wasted in petty concerns, injured by conceptual analysis or lost in micromanaging.

TSO    WANG

SITTING DOWN	FORGETTING
SITUATED/RESTING	OBLIVIOUS OF
SEAT/PLACE	NEGLECT/LOSE
ON THE GROUND	VANISHING/HIDING

OPENING THE WAY TO EXPERIENCING THE CONTINUAL ABUNDANCE OF ESSENTIAL/EARTHLY TAO BY:

DIVESTING AND EMPTYING THE HEART-MIND OF EMOTIONAL OBJECT-'GOODS'.
RELINQUISHING OF EMOTIONALLY/AFFECTIVELY PREFERRING, INVESTING IN, ACQUIRING, ATTACHING TO, CLAIMING, OWNING AND RETAINING EXPERIENTIAL PHENOMENA.
STEPPING ASIDE AND LETTING EXPERIENTIAL PHENOMENA GO JUST *AS* THEY HAVE PRESENTED THEMSELVES TO CONSCIOUS AWARENESS WITHOUT GRASPING, HOLDING ONTO AND CLINGING TO THEM.
EQUALLY MIRRORING, REFLECTING, SUBTRACTING, ABANDONING, CENTERING, VOIDING, RELEASING AND ELIMINATING EXPERIENTIAL PHENOMENA JUST *AS* THEY HAVE PRESENTED THEMSELVES TO CONSCIOUS AWARENESS.

RECORD TWO
Equalizing Matters Discoursing

CH'I

齊

E<small>VEN</small>/<small>EQUAL</small>
U<small>NIFORM</small>/<small>ALL ALIKE</small>
A<small>RRANGE</small>/<small>LINE UP</small>
R<small>EGULAR</small>/<small>HARMONIOUS</small>

WU

物

M<small>ATTER</small>/<small>PHYSICAL</small>/<small>MATERIAL</small>
T<small>HINGS</small>/<small>OBJECTS</small>/<small>ENTITIES</small>
M<small>ATTERS OUTSIDE OF ONESELF</small>
A<small>FFAIRS OF THE WORLD</small>

LUN

論

D<small>ISCUSS</small>/<small>DISCOURSE</small>
S<small>PEAK OF</small>
E<small>SSAY</small>/<small>THEORY</small>
R<small>EASON</small>

RECORD TWO
Equalizing Matters Discoursing

Central Themes

The second Record of the *Nei P'ien* is about bipolarity, reciprocating, interchangeability, relativity, equality and oneness.

Distinctions are made between Heaven-Earth and human being, Spirit and body, Higher Mind and ego-mind and Great Understanding and Words and little understanding and words. Great Understanding and Words are broad, clear, slow and calm and little understanding and words are narrow, confused, busy and frantic.

The subjective ego-mind makes and proliferates endless abstractions, objectifications, conceptual discriminations, linguistic categorizations and theoretical formulations that result in countless debates, contentions, arguments and strife that never return to their Origin/Tao. Autonomous ego-states have no apparent ruler or executive ego to organize them. Original Higher Mind is a nondual Tao-like bipolar unity that precedes and is beyond dualistic oppositions and judgments such as true-false, good-bad, right-wrong, gain-loss and their subjective, relative and limited perspectives.

The human body is transient, grows, declines, deteriorates, degenerates and dies. The Human Spirit is infinite-eternal, immortal and free. Human beings are firmly attached and clinging to their muddled views and entrenched positions, busily involved in excessive and futile pursuits, deeply entangled and lost in the laborious and exhausting strivings and strugglings of their confused knowings and fruitless doings. Human beings only blow on flutes while Heaven exists like a vital cosmic wind blowing through Nature's hollow spaces individualizing all beings and things.

Things are the myriad objects of the subjective ego-mind and are comprised of innumerable alternating, reversing and interchanging dualities within human existence and experience. Constant Tao is not an object-thing and is beyond all this-that dualities; being formless, boundless, limitless, ineffable and nameless. Constant Tao is the Nondual Unity, Heavenly Equality and True Master that unifies and equalizes all beings and things and their realities, distinctions, partialities and activities.

True human beings are true to their inner Tao-nature/Virtuosity/Te, are relying upon the Clear Light and Pivotal Axis of Tao, are identifying *as* Heavenly Tao's Equality and are unifying, equalizing and harmonizing distinctions and dualities. They are not objectifying beings and things, not construing limits and definitions, and are not making right-wrong discriminations and judgments or having good-bad valuations and preferences that result in a loss of Constant Tao. True human beings are not speculating, theorizing and debating about the reality and nature of Tao, the operations of the universe or the ultimate reality and absolute truth of knowledge.

True human beings are identifying with non-knowing and are maintaining doubt, uncertainty, healthy skepticism and clarity about knowledge due to the context-relevant, situation-specific, perspective-dependent and standpoint-relative nature of 'knowing'. Their understanding goes far beyond ordinary knowledge and the ambiguous, paradoxical, transposable, variable and transient dualities of subjective ego-mind; even those of being and non-being, reality-dream, truth-delusion, acceptable-unacceptable and life-death.

Some True human beings are supernatural beings whose Virtuosity/Te makes them invulnerable and immune to external influences and harm and capable of ascending flights into transcendent and non-ordinary states of higher consciousness beyond the space-time limitations of ordinary ego-mind and the physical world. They are beings of far-reaching vision who are living in the simplicity of unity, equality and harmony; are wandering in realms before there were beings and things and living and dying and are merging with the cosmos, natural world and all of life in the universe.

True human beings are letting everyone and everything be who and what they uniquely are and are accepting them just *as* they are being and changing without interfering with them. They are embodying and personifying Great Virtuosity/Te and the clear, imageless and shadowless precious and radiant Light of Tao. True human beings are Heaven's Reservoir and Treasury and the Great Awakening of Human Being.

2-1 ❖ THE MUSIC OF HEAVEN

TEXT

A Tao-Master is sitting down, gazing skyward and breathing slowly and deeply in a trance-like state of consciousness. A disciple is asking, 'What is this? Your body is like a withered tree and your mind like dead ashes. You are not the same person you were a moment ago.' The Tao-Master replies, 'Yes, just now I lost consciousness of myself. Understand? You know the flute music of human beings and probably the music of Earth but not the music of Heaven.'

The disciple asks for elaboration and the Tao-Master continues, 'The universe blows a vital cosmic breath we call wind. When active, sounds are emitted from the myriad openings in Nature, from high mountain crevices to deep cavern hollows. Sounds are made like rushing waters, whistling arrows, sighing, moaning, wailing, howling, rustling, hissing. Gentle breezes make faint harmonies and strong winds make loud choruses. This is the music of Earth.'

The disciple asks about the music of Heaven. The Tao-Master continues, 'The music of Heaven is the same cosmic wind blowing through the myriad different openings so that they each make their own unique sounds. Only Heaven is creating these absolutely unique sounds.'[11]

Commentary

True attenders are:

Experiencing that stilling the will of impulses, emptying the heart of desires and clearing the mind of concepts are enabling them to experience states and realms of non-ordinary consciousness.

Attuning to the vital Yin Ch'i/Yang Ch'i energies that are originating, forming and manifesting the unique individualities and Virtuosity/Te of human beings.

Opening to and allowing the natural spontaneous/Tzu Jan 'playing' of Tao as it is presencing the myriad experiential phenomena/Wan Wu within conscious awareness and the attending relationship/process.

2-2 ❖ Broad and Narrow

Text

Great Understanding is wide and spacious and small knowledge is narrow and limited. Great Speech is clear and concise and small talk is chatty and verbose.

When asleep, our Spiritual energy wanders freely. When awake, our bodily senses take over and we become entangled in various distracting worldly activities and strivings. Sometimes we are innocent and transparent and other times, secretive and deceptive. Minor fears are causing anxiety and major ones are causing panic. Words fly out of our mouths like arrows as if we absolutely know what is right and wrong. We cling to our cherished viewpoints and opinions without realizing that they are as impermanent as the seasons.

Our vital energies dwindle, decay and dissolve daily, caught in a one-way current, drowning in our own doings and never circulating and returning to our Source. Stopped up, crushed down; we grow old, sealed in our excesses, and spiral downward toward death with no hope of recovering, restoring and renewing life.

COMMENTARY

True attenders are:

Experiencing the differences between the inwardness, depth, spaciousness, clarity and conciseness of great understanding and true dialogue and the sense-bound, ego-invested knowings, talkings and distractions of ordinary human consciousness, activities and strivings.

Experiencing deep compassion for the ordinary ego-mind states, intrapsychic and interpersonal conflicts, defense mechanisms and coping strategies of human beings who are enmeshed and entangled with the things, objects and others in their daily lives.

Identifying *as* the spacious and all-encompassing perspective of Tao as they diligently assist human beings as they are undergoing some of the painful vicissitudes of the human condition, e.g., anxiety, depression, fear, panic, judgments, excesses, exhaustion, incapacitation, life-threatening deterioration, impermanence and dying.

2-3 ❖ ONE AND MANY

TEXT

Joy-anger, happiness-sadness, hope-fear, strength-weakness, humility-aggression, enthusiasm-regret---all arising from hollowness, fungi from dampness, continually appearing, alternating and disappearing like day and night. Let them be! Let them be!

All of our many emotions are experienced as 'mine', but who knows from where and how they originate. There seems to be some True Master with an identity and actions but no form that can be found.

All of our separate body parts work together, but which ones are in charge; one of them, some of them, all of them, none of them? Are they all servants or do they each take turns governing each other? Whether or not a True Master is discovered, it neither adds to nor takes away from its reality and truth.

COMMENTARY

True attenders are:

Regarding the myriad bipolar feelings, thoughts and actions of human beings as continually alternating within human existence and experience and are simply letting them be and do so.

Understanding that, although incapable of being experienced as one object among others, Tao-Self is the True Ruler and True Master of all of the many separate and diverse ego-structures, processes, functions, activities and states of human existence, consciousness and experience.

Trusting in the reality, truth and actuality of Tao's identity and agency and the potency and efficacy of its Virtuosity/Te present and operating in the attending relationship/process without needing cognitive empirical verification.

2-4 ❖ LIVING AND DYING

TEXT

Once given our body, we are attaching to it and its natural existing and functioning until the ending of our lives. We persist through struggling against things or conforming to them and run our life course like unstoppable galloping horses. How sad!

We toil and sweat all of our lives without seeing any real results. We exhaust ourselves without rest or relaxation. What a pity! We say, 'At least I am not dead' but what good is that?

Our bodies decay, our minds deteriorate, our Souls decline and our Spirit degenerates. What a great sorrow! Is our human life really this absurd? Am I the only one who sees the absurdity? Do you see it too?

COMMENTARY

True attenders are:

Having deep compassion for human beings who are attached to, and completely identified with, their physical bodies, mental states, emotional feelings and ego-activities as they are undergoing and dealing with the processes and experiences of living and dying in their lives.

Observing correspondences between human living and dying and the life of the attending relationship/process, e.g., the resisting and struggling and/or the cooperating and collaborating of human beings.

Observing that some professional colleagues are striving for referrals, toiling long hours, sweating out income, suffering burn-out, depleting their vital energy, compromising their Spiritual integrity and even resorting to unethical practices, e.g., in the solicitation, manipulation and retention of human beings. What a great sorrow! Do not they see the absurdity?

2-5 ❖ RIGHT AND WRONG

TEXT

Being true to ourselves and making our Original Mind a teacher, we all, both the wise and the foolish, have a True Teacher. When we are not being true to ourselves and are making and choosing between right and wrong judgments, it is like leaving today and arriving yesterday, i.e., making something exist that does not exist. Even sages are not able to do this much less ordinary people.

COMMENTARY

True attenders are:

Being true to themselves and following their innermost, deepest, centermost, truest and utmost Tao-nature/Virtuosity/Te and are taking Original Mind as their True Teacher.

Experiencing that human beings engaged in the attending relationship/process also have an Original Mind and True Teacher, regardless of their degree of consciousness and extent of development.

Not attempting to intellectually assess, evaluate, understand and judge the change and transformation process in terms of either correctly or incorrectly made and/or timed interpretations, interactions and interventions and, rather, are trusting in the validity of its natural unfolding, proceeding, developing and completing.

2-6 ❖ Absolute and Relative

Text

Speaking words is not just blowing air. Words have meaning but their meaning is not constant. So, do words say something, anything, everything or nothing? Are they more or less meaningful than the chirping of birds?[12]

Can Tao be so lost that we conceive of trueness and falseness? Can words be so lost that we speak about rightness and wrongness? How can Tao not exist and words not have meaning? The reality of Tao is lost in abstractions, objectifications and limited understanding and the meaning of words is lost in flowery rhetoric, oration and contending schools of thought.

What one school of thought is deeming right, another one is deeming wrong and vice versa. Bringing the Truth to Light through Clarity is wronging the rights and righting the wrongs.

Commentary

True attenders are:
Using words that are natural and spontaneous expressions of the reality and truth of their Tao-natures/Virtuosity/Te in the moment; have no absolutely fixed meanings and change with the context, form and process of the attending relationship.

Con-versing (turning together) with human beings without necessarily intellectually and analytically discriminating what they are speaking into dualistic judgments and valuations of what is good-bad and right-wrong that are obscuring the reality of Tao and the meaning of words.

Not engaging in the rhetoric and politic of contending schools of psychotherapy/counseling and are harmoniously integrating them in the Light and Clarity of Nondual Tao.

2-7 ❖ THIS AND THAT

TEXT

Everything can be either a 'this' or a 'that'. That is coming from this and this is coming from that. This and that are giving rise to each other. I experience my this and your that.

The unities of Heaven-Earth and the 10,000 things cannot be affirmed nor negated by their different characteristics.

Death, wrong and unacceptable are arising from life, right and acceptable. True human beings are not bothering with such dualistic conceptual distinctions and are illuminating everything in the Clear Light of Heavenly Tao. They are understanding that every this is also a that and vice versa and that they both are, at times, right and wrong.

No distinctions between reciprocal complements are the essential Axis and Pivot of Nondual Tao. At this still center-point, True human beings are observing the infinite in all things and their endless bipolar interchangings and transformings. Apparent mutually exclusive dualistic opposites are a single Unity when seen in the Clear Light of Tao.

COMMENTARY

True attenders are:

Experiencing that their Tao-state of being is beyond mutually arising and interchangeable this-that dualities and that all experiential phenomena in the attending relationship/process are nondualistic bipolar unities.

Understanding that all nondualistic bipolar unities are not mutually exclusive opposites but are mutually interdependent, reciprocally interchangeable and corresponding complements as in all Yin/Yang Ch'i dynamically alternating interrelationships.

Conducting the attending relationship/process from a harmoniously centered position that is the Pivotal Axis and Clear Light of Tao enabling them to experience the essential unity and constancy of all of its many individual and endlessly changing and interchanging experiential phenomena.

2-8 ❖ Acceptable and Unacceptable

Text

What is acceptable and unacceptable is what we are deeming as acceptable and unacceptable. A way is a way by wayfarers making it so. The myriad things are so or not so because we are identifying them as so or not so. Why is this so or not so? Because it is so or not so!

Everything has its unique inherent nature and function and there is no-thing that is not so or not acceptable, e.g., stalks and columns, lepers and beauties, familiar and strange things; and all are One in Tao. Separateness and difference are their unique existence and their union and identity are their dissolution. Separating, uniting and dissolving are the reality and process of all things.

True human beings are understanding the identity and interchangeability of all things; do not dwell in divisions, distinctions and differences and naturally unify everything in One Constant Tao. Constancy is being useful and utility is realizing our innermost, deepest, centermost, truest and utmost Tao-nature/Virtuosity/Te and following the natural course of things that bring happiness and completion without our even knowing why or how it is so.

COMMENTARY

True attenders are:

Understanding the individual human beings engaged in, and the myriad separate and different experiential phenomena of, the attending relationship/process on their own unique terms but also are contextualizing them in the superordinate encompassing and unifying framework and perspective of Tao.

Co-creating the attending relationship/process by considering it to be so and acceptable based upon its unique nature, conduct and function and by participating in it as such with the human beings engaged in it.

Unifying, harmonizing and dissolving differences in psychotherapy/counseling approaches in One Constant Tao and are not making conceptual distinctions and methodolgical variations through actualizing their Tao-nature/Virtuosity/Te, following the natural course and unfolding of the attending relationship/process and assisting in unself-consciously allowing it to naturally reach an appropriate, acceptable and happy completion.

2-9 ❖ THREE IN THE MORNING

TEXT

Exhausting our Spirit trying to unify things without remembering that they already are One is called 'Three in the Morning'. A monkey keeper is handing out nuts to the monkeys. 'You are getting three nuts this morning and four in the evening.' The monkeys are all furious. 'Okay, four nuts this morning and three in the evening.' The monkeys are all happy.

The total number of nuts is the same in both instances but the different arrangement results in either anger or happiness. In the same way, True human beings are identifying with the One Reality of Tao behind the outward differences while attuning to the inherent nature of beings. They are harmonizing both right and wrong and are residing in the Heavenly Equality of

Tao, the balance of Nature. This is the dual Unity of walking two roads at once.

Commentary

True attenders are:

Not exhausting their vital Spiritual energy/Ch'i trying to unify the myriad apparent dualities, dichotomies and paradoxes of experiential phenomena but are simply realizing their bipolar unity and identity as manifestations of One Constant Tao and its dynamically interchangeable Yin Ch'i/Yang Ch'i energies and forms.

Recognizing the need for consistent structure but are not necessarily concerning themselves with fundamentally inconsequential issues in the attending relationship/process, e.g., whether fees are paid before or after the meeting, whether issues from last meeting are followed up with, whether next appointments are scheduled at the end of the meeting or later in the week, etc..

Appreciating the 'grist for the mill' of analyzing and interpreting any and all content or behavior but are typically harmonizing interchangeable differences in the attending relationship/process, e.g., who sits where, begins the meeting, keeps track of time, ends the meeting, gets up off their chair first, etc. by residing in the Heavenly Constancy, Unity and Equality of Tao while everything else is changing in the ways that it does.

2-10 ❖ Loss and Completion

Text

In ancient times, understanding is so profound that it reaches back to a time when no-thing exists and is so complete that no-thing can be added to it. Then come sages who know that things exist but make no distinctions between them. Next come human beings who make distinctions between things but do not name them. Then come human beings who name things but do not evaluate or judge them to be good or bad, right or wrong. Then come people who evaluate and judge things to be good or bad, right or wrong.

When judgments and valuations are being made, Tao is lost in abstractions, objectifications, desires, preferences and exclusions that prevent its completion within human existence, consciousness and experience. But are there such things as losing or completing? There is neither one when a master musician is not playing an instrument, a master conductor is not waving a baton or a master logician is not discussing a theory. When it comes to Tao, True human beings are not making such conceptual distinctions, are following the natural course of things, are accepting things as they are and are identifying *as* Constant Tao and its Clear Light.

Commentary

True attenders are:

Identifying *as* the primordial undifferentiated and ultimate-less Non-Being/Wu Chi of Tao and are not making and naming dualistic distinctions, judgments, valuations and preferences about the experiential phenomena occurring in the attending relationship/process.

Observing that many of their professional colleagues are working within some kind of object-ifying, dualistic, discriminating, labeling, judgmental and preferential conceptual-theoretical framework usually involving psychopathological classifications, psychodiagnostic categorizations and related psychotherapy treatment models.

Not displacing or eclipsing the Clear Light of Tao with desirable and preferred diagnostic assessments, case formulations, treatment plans, intervention strategies and outcome objectives and are, rather, accepting, allowing and following the natural unfolding of the course of the attending relationship/process and the spontaneous presencing of its experiential phenomena with a wide variety of human beings, with a wide variety of clinical issues and with a wide variety of treatment possibilities and options.

2-11 ❖ SOMETHING AND NOTHING

TEXT

Now, I am going to say something about all of this. But I do not know what category it falls under or whether or not it is even relevant here. Nonetheless, it must be relevant somewhere at sometime to somebody and so it is not different from the statements that others make that do fall into some category. So, here it is!

There is a beginning. There is no beginning of that beginning. There is no beginning of that no beginning of beginning. There is being. There is nonbeing. There is no beginning of that nonbeing. There is no beginning of that no beginning of nonbeing. Suddenly, there are being and nonbeing.

But I do not really know which is being and which is nonbeing. And now, I have just said something but I do not really know whether what I have said has really said something or whether it has not said something.

COMMENTARY

True attenders are:

Understanding that the originating of human beings is an essential Mystery far antedating their physical incarnation, personal history, the etiology of their psychological condition, the onset of their presenting issues and their initiation of the attending relationship/process.

Taking conceptualizations and verbalizations made by human beings openly and lightly with an attitude and approach of non-knowing if they really are or are not what they appear to be because of being context-relevant, situation-specific, perspective-dependent and standpoint-relative.

Understanding that notions of human being and living, health, change, growth, development, transformation, evolution, etc. are not absolute or universal, since they also are context-relevant, situation-specific, perspective-dependent and standpoint-relative.

2-12 ❖ UNITY AND MULTIPLICITY

TEXT

Nothing in the world is larger than a hair tip or smaller than a Sacred mountain. No one is living longer than a stillborn child and a thousand year old human being dies young. Heaven, Earth, I and the myriad things are all born at the same time and are all One. Since everything is One, what else is there to say?

But I just said that we are all One. One and what I said about it make two and two and One make three. Continuing in this way, even a mathematician cannot calculate the ending. If moving from Nonbeing to Being, we reach three; how far will we go from being to being? Enough! It is time to stop the whole endless process and to just let things be *as* they are.

COMMENTARY

True attenders are:

Understanding that the experiential phenomena of the attending relationship/process are a paradoxical unity, e.g., seemingly minor events can be profoundly meaningful and seemingly major ones can be relatively insignificant and seemingly dead issues may persist and seemingly chronic ones may desist.

Experiencing that there is no end to the identification and proliferation of phenomena, associations, connections, interrelationships, etc. occurring throughout the attending relationship/process.

Simply letting all of the many, diverse and rich experiential phenomena occurring throughout the attending relationship/process just be *as* they are.

2-13 ❖ DISCRIMINATING AND EMBRACING

TEXT

Tao is without limits and speech has no constancy. Using words is creating limiting discriminations, distinctions, definitions, classifications, theories, debates, competitions and contentions.

True human beings are embracing and accepting what is beyond the realm of Heaven-Earth and the universe and are discussing. Regarding what is within the realm of Heaven-Earth and the universe, True human beings are discussing but are not making discriminations nor passing judgment.

When there are discriminating and discussing; there is something beyond both. True human beings are embracing all things equally while ordinary people are displaying, debating and defending their discriminations and failing to see clearly.

COMMENTARY

True attenders are:

Experiencing that using words is creating conceptul distinctions, diagnostic classifications, theoretical categories, separate schools and movements and professional debates in the field of psychotherapy/counseling.

Accepting and not discriminating, discussing or debating the transphenomenal reality and phenomenal actuality of Tao in the attending relationship/process.

Observing that many colleagues are continually theorizing; discussing and debating about constituents, factors, variables and contingencies in psychotherapy/counseling work and are displaying and defending their discriminations and judgments with clinical observations, evidence-based research findings and empirical data published in professional journals and presented at professional conferences.

2-14 ❖ Square and Round

Text

Great Tao is not being named and Great Discriminations are not being worded. Great Benevolence, Modesty and Courage are, respectively, beyond good deeds, humble behavior and daring bravery. These five are essentially perfect, round and Heavenly.

Tao being objectified is not Tao. Worded discriminations, invested good-doing, compulsive deference and risky behavior are, respectively, not sufficient, universal, trustworthy and complete. These five, existentially, have become imperfect, square and Earthly.

Commentary

True attenders are:

Not objectifying Tao or necessarily naming and labeling its myriad differential manifestations in the attending relationship/process using psychiatric nomenclature, nosological classifications and psychological jargon.

Experiencing that the essential reality of true discernment, genuine kindness, respectful appreciation and committed engagement are beyond fine words, good deeds, retiring demeanor and risk-taking.

Experiencing that the essential reality of authentic discrimination, benevolence, modesty and courage can become inauthentically expressed through the adoption of a professional persona of astuteness, competency, courtesy and confidence.

2-15 ❖ Wording and Not-Wording

Text

Knowing that we do not know is perfect understanding. Understanding discriminations not made and worded and Tao not conceptualized and named are Heaven's Reservoir and

Treasury. Poured into, it is never filled and poured out of, it is never emptied. Its source of supply is unknown. This is the precious hidden Light of Tao.

Commentary

True attenders are:

Understanding that true understanding in the attending relationship/process is founded in the non-knowing and non-wording of that which is beyond knowing and wording, i.e., Tao and Mystery, and not necessarily in the worded concepts, definitions, theories and formulations of traditional and conventional schools of psychotherapy/counseling.

Attuning to, opening to and drawing from the energetic Reservoir and Treasury of Heaven's Tao, the all-receiving and all-giving, inexhaustible source of, and abundant re-source for, the agency, potency and efficacy of the attending relationship/process.

Embodying, personifying and identifying *as* the precious Hidden Light of Tao; their innermost, deepest, centermost, truest and utmost Tao-nature/Virtuosity/Te, that is conducting, facilitating, guiding, developing and completing the attending relationship/process.

2-16 ❖ Trying and Letting-Go

Text

One ruler is saying to another ruler, 'I have been wanting to attack these three neighboring states ever since I became ruler but why am I not doing so?' The other ruler answers, 'Those three states are small, poor and desolate. Why bother! A very long time ago, ten suns rose simultaneously and the myriad beings were all illuminated. How much greater is Virtuosity than these suns!'

COMMENTARY

True attenders are:

Awed and humbled by, and grateful for, however they are understanding and whenever they are experiencing the greatness and vastness of the efficacious power of their Virtuosity/Te present and operating in the attending relationship/process.

Identifying *as* the magnitude and magnificence of their inner Tao-nature/Virtuosity/Te and the availability, accessibility and utility of the power of its gifts, talents and genius to accept, encourage, support, assist, facilitate, guide and benefit needful human beings as they are being in their own lives.

Not necessarily depleting or wasting the vital energy/Ch'i of their Virtuosity/Te by attacking rather than accepting some of the minor symptoms, petty concerns and little problems of the small ego-states of human beings.

2-17 ❖ Knowing and Not-Knowing

Text

A disciple is asking a Tao-Master, 'Do you know what is common to all beings?' The Tao-Master replies, 'How can I know that?' The disciple then asks, 'Do you know that you do not know?' The Tao-Master again replies, 'How can I know that?' Persisting, the disciple asks, 'Then does anyone know anything?' The Tao-Master, yet again, replies, 'How can I know that? But let me say this. How do you know that if I say that I know, I really do not know and when I say that I do not know, that I really do know?

Now I will ask you a few questions. People staying in damp places have aching bones but do eels? People living in high trees have falling fears but do monkeys? Who knows the right place? People eat meat, deers eat grass, owls eat mice and snakes eat centipedes. Who knows the right food? Monkeys mate with monkeys, elk and deer run together and eels play with fishes. Who knows the right companion? Women considered beautiful by people scare off birds, fish and animals. Who knows what is attractive? The standards of good and bad, right and wrong are relative and so confused, how can we know which is which?'

The disciple then inquires, 'If you cannot distinguish between them, can True human beings do so?' The Tao-Master answers, 'True human beings are Spirit-like. Blazing swamps, icy rivers and quaking lands cannot burn, freeze or frighten them. They ride clouds and mist, mount the sun and moon and wander far beyond this world. Living and dying do not affect them much less distinctions of good-bad, right-wrong and gain-loss.'

COMMENTARY

True attenders are:

Understanding that knowing is relative and uncertain; are not knowing whether or not their observations of human beings are generalizable or whether or not their understandings are good or right and are trusting that meeting with human beings in the context of the attending relationship/process is a good and right place in which to be.

Identifying *as* Tao-Spirit, are unaffected by the Yin/Yang Ch'i fluctuations of bipolar experiential phenomena and are experiencing immunity to physical harm and psychological wounding in the attending relationship/process.

Able to freely wander in the uncharted and unmapped vastness of non-ordinary states of consciousness beyond the finite limitations of ego-identification and the attending relationship/process and are relatively unimpeded by concerns about the goodness or rightness of interpretations, interactions and interventions.

2-18 ❖ DREAMING AND AWAKENING

TEXT

A disciple is asking a Tao-Master, 'I heard from Confucius[13] that True human beings are not involved in worldly affairs, do not pursue gain or avoid loss and do not seek renown or anything else, not even Tao. They say something by their silence and nothing by their words and wander far beyond this dusty world. Are such True human beings personifying the Mysterious workings of Tao?' The Tao-Master replies, 'You are too quick in your conclusions. You see an unhatched egg and hear a rooster crowing. You see an unstrung bow and smell a duck roasting.'

The Tao-Master continues, 'True human beings are accompanying sun and moon, embracing space and time, uniting with everything, interfering with nothing, ignoring confusions, honoring the lowly and acting naturally and spontaneously without busyness or struggling. They are experiencing the myriad ages and beings simply as one whole, are accepting everything as what it is and are allowing everything to do what it does.

How do I know that loving life is not a delusion or whether a person facing death is not like an exile who forgot the way home? A woman taken captive by a ruler weeps profusely but after living in the palace regrets having cried. How do I know that the dead do not regret longing for birth and clinging to life? People dreaming of a feast may weep the next morning. People dreaming of weeping may enjoy a feast the next day.

When we are dreaming, we do not know we are dreaming and in the dream may even interpret the dream. Only after waking do we know that we were dreaming. Only after a Great Awakening will we know that this life has been one great dream. All the while, people think that they are awake, believing that they know themselves and understand things, calling this person 'leader' and that one 'follower'. How dense! And Confucius, you and I are each dreaming too. These words may sound like double talk but after many generations, a Great Being may arrive who explains the reality and truth of it all. Or it could happen at any time now!'

Commentary

True attenders are:

Ignoring the confusions of various psychotherapy/counseling approaches; are empathizing with every kind of experience in the attending relationship/process; are not objectifying, pathologizing, stigmatizing, marginalizing, infantilizing, patronizing, criminalizing, demonizing and otherwise dehumanizing human beings and are not interfering with the natural and spontaneous unfolding, proceeding, developing and completing of the attending relationship/process.

Not seeking personal outcomes, professional reputation or financial gain; are abiding by but not limited by conventional rules, ranks, roles and rituals and are open to non-ordinary states of consciousness and nondual realities that are far beyond those typically experienced in traditional psychotherapy/counseling practice.

Accepting the subjective and paradoxical nature of human existence, the relativity of reality and actuality, the interchangeability of reality and dreaming, the epistemological limits of knowing and empathizing and are anticipating a shift in consciousness and a collective awakening that will reveal the dream-like and fantasy-like nature of ordinary human living.

2-19 ❖ Winning and Losing

Text

The Tao-Master continues, 'Suppose you and I are debating. If you win and I lose, are you right and am I wrong? Or vice versa? Is one of us right or wrong or are both of us right or wrong or are neither one of us right or wrong? If you and I do not know, should we ask someone else to judge? But what if they agree or disagree with you or me or both of us? How can they be objective? If you, I or others cannot decide, should we wait for yet another? Waiting for changing opinions is like waiting for nothing.

Seeing everything in relation to the Heavenly Unity and Equality of Tao leaves differing viewpoints just as they are and enables us to live out our years harmoniously. This means understanding that what we consider being and right may not be so.

But if they truly are so, they will be so different from nonbeing and wrong that there is no real debating. Forget such conventional distinctions and live out your years in the boundless and limitless and make them your Home!'.

Commentary

True attenders are:

Generally considering it irrelevant, pointless and unproductive to debate about whether interpretations, interactions and interventions in the attending relationship/process are right or wrong, which is usually so obvious that outside consultation is unnecessary.

Harmonizing all dualities and activities in the attending relationship/process in the Unity and Equality of Heavenly Tao and are usually leaving all differing distinctions, everchanging viewpoints and value judgments just as they are rather than attempting to determine whether they are really real, true and right or not.

Forgetting conventional assessments of and judgments about the unique reality, integral unity and relative veracity of the attending relationship/process and are allowing its harmonious completion through being and living the openness, spaciousness and vastness of Tao.

2-20 ❖ Light and Shadow

Text

Shade is saying to Shadow, 'A while ago you were moving, then standing still and then sitting down and now you are standing up. Why all of this inconsistency?' Shadow answers, 'I depend upon others to be and to move. And others depend upon something else to be who they are and to do what they do. It is all natural, like a snake depends upon its scales or a cicada depends upon its wings. How can I control or know why I do this or that?'

Commentary

True attenders are:

Being perfectly responsive to the mutually interdependent realities, intersubjective actualities and correlated experiences of the attending relationship/process.

Aligning with, attuning to and according with human beings in a co-creative, cooperative and collaborative attending relationship/process of mutuality, equality and reciprocity.

Experiencing the naturalness, vitality, origin-ality and spontaneity of the true attending relationship/process as phenomena naturally presence into awareness, awareness naturally flows into activity and activity naturally completes itself, like the correspondence of changing light and shifting shadow.

2-21 ❖ Chuang Tzu and a Butterfly

Text

I, Chuang Tzu, am dreaming that I am a butterfly, happily flitting and fluttering about enjoying being alive without knowing who I am. Suddenly, I wake up and realize that I am indeed Chuang Tzu. But now, I do not know if I was dreaming that I was a butterfly or I am a butterfly dreaming that I am Chuang Tzu. There is the same difference between us. This is the transforming of beings and things.

Commentary

True attenders are:

Regarding waking and dreaming as states of consciousness that, phenomenologically, are equally real, valid and interchangeable depending upon relative perspectives.

Experiencing that; while they are separate, distinct and different from the human beings with whom they are meeting; at times, it is difficult to discern who is the so-called psychotherapist/counselor and who is the so-called patient/counselee.

Awakening from dreaming, fantasizing and imagining the phenomenal realities and actualities of the attending relationship/process into experiencing their natural concept-free, name-free and role-free interchangeability, reciprocity and transforming within the contextual Unity and Identity of Tao.

YUAN	YU

ORIGIN SOURCE TRULY/ACTUALLY MATTER OF COURSE	SWIM/FLOAT TRAVEL AROUND SAUNTER/STROLL ROAM/ROVE

OPENING THE WAY TO EXPERIENCING THE CONTINUOUS CREATIVITY OF ULTIMATE/ORIGINAL TAO BY:

ORIGINATING AND SOURCING OBJECT-'DEEDS' AT THE WELLSPRINGS/HEADWATERS OF VOLITIONAL CONATIVE ACTIVITIES.
NOT STRATEGIZING, ADVANCING, IMPLEMENTING, EXECUTING, CONCLUDING, COUNTERACTING AND RESISTING EXPERIENTIAL PHENOMENA.
STEPPING UP AND GOING WITH EXPERIENTIAL PHENOMENA JUST *AS* THEY ARE UNFOLDING WITHOUT CONTROLLING, FORCING AND MANIPULATING THEM.
HAPPILY SUPPORTING, ASSISTING, FACILITATING, COMPLYING WITH, FOLLOWING, FLOWING ALONG WITH, RESPONDING TO AND RECREATING WITH EXPERIENTIAL PHENOMENA.

RECORD THREE
Nourishing Life's Host

YANG

Nourish
Care for/support/maintain
Rear/bring up/raise

SHENG

Birth/be born/bear
Beget/bring forth/produce
Life/living

CHU

主

Lord/ruler
Host/principal
Master/owner

RECORD THREE
Nourishing Life's Host

Central Themes

The third Record of the *Nei P'ien* is about energy, vitality, centrality, harmony, nourishing and Spirit.

True human beings are going by Constant Tao; are not pursuing knowledge, name or fame and are centered in and following the middle way between extremes. They are nourishing and conserving their vital life energies/Ch'i, are preserving the integrity and harmony of their Virtuosity/Te and are increasing their immunity and longevity.

In their activities, True human beings are intuitively moved and guided by Spirit, are going along with the natural Yin Ch'i/Yang Ch'i interchanging dynamic and Wu Wei Ch'i flowing kinetic operations of Heavenly Tao and are following the natural constitution and structures of the world body. They are moving freely in and through the open spaces between things, are taking the path of least resistance and are following natural grains and riding energy currents. The activities of True human beings are non-resistive, yielding, seamless, frictionless and effortless and are not depleting or exhausting. When moving in and through solid structures, they are doing so with alertness, slowness, carefulness and subtleness.

True human beings are allowing, attuning to, according with, following and cooperating with the vital energies, life forces and life-streaming rhythms of Ch'i which they are consciously cultivating, conserving, compounding and circulating. They are caring for and nourishing the life of Spirit, Nature, beings and human beings.

True human beings are experiencing that Heavenly Tao gives life and constitution to beings, are honoring their unique Spirit and are not hiding from the reality of their Heaven-endowed (en-Tao-ed) life, Tao-natures and Virtuosity/Te. They are accepting that beings come into and go out of life because life follows along and everything passes on endlessly. True human beings are content with their time, are willing to follow along and are living freely beyond the joy and grief of birth and death, just as does the eternal fireflaming of Spirit.

3-1 ❖ Following the Middle Way

Text

Our lives are limited but true knowledge is unlimited. Using our limited lives to pursue limitless knowledge is exhausting and dangerous. If doing good, be avoiding fame and if not doing good, be avoiding blame. By keeping to the Central Axis and Pivot of Constant Tao and following the Middle Way, we can conserve vitality, preserve integrity, nourish intimacy and enjoy longevity.

Commentary

True attenders are:

Not pursuing the Reality of Tao and its operations with their relatively limited ego-minds and mortally finite lives which can only attain a transient rational, intellectual and conceptual understanding of Tao.

Not motivated by gaining fame and avoiding blame in the conducting of the attending relationship/process by doing 'good' or being 'right' in their interpretations, interactions and interventions.

Centered in the Pivotal Axis of Tao; are allowing and following the middle coursing of the attending relationship/process; are sustaining the vitality and maintaining the integrity of their Virtuosity/Te and its efficacious potency and are nourishing the being and lives of human beings and the life of the attending relationship/process.

3-2 ❖ Frictionless Activity

Text

A ruler's cook is butchering an ox. Every planting of her feet, turning of her knee, thrusting of her hip, leaning of her shoulder, bending of her arm and guiding of her hand; the singing of the knife and the slicing of the flesh; are all attuned in perfect rhythm like a smoothly flowing dance. The ruler is remarking, 'You accomplish your work with such skillful technique!'

The cook lays down her knife and replies, 'What I care about is Tao, which is far beyond technique or skill. When I first began this work, I see nothing but the whole ox. After several years, I see the contours of the parts of the ox. Now, I am working intuitively by Spirit and not my eyes. My senses are not operating and Spirit is taking over and guiding me.

I am following the natural structures, letting the knife find its way through the cavities and along the crevices, never touching a ligament or tendon, much less a joint or bone. A good cook is changing his knife yearly because he cuts and an average cook is changing his knife monthly because he hacks. I have been using this knife for nineteen years and carved thousands of oxen, yet the blade is still as sharp as when it was new.

There are open spaces between the joints and the knife blade is very thin. Inserting what has no thickness into what is spacious, there is plenty of room for the knife to play without friction or wear. That is why the knife is still sharp as ever. Whenever I am coming to a difficult place, I carefully size it up, stay concentrated on what I am doing and move the knife very slowly and carefully. The piece just comes apart and falls off. Then I am just standing there, knife in hand, looking around and feeling satisfied, and then wiping the knifeblade clean and setting it down.'

'Splendid!', exclaims the ruler. 'You have shown me how to nourish life!'

Commentary

True attenders are:

According with Tao and its Yin Ch'i/Yang Ch'i reciprocating dynamics and Wu Wei Ch'i flowing kinetics and are conducting the attending relationship/process as a rhythmically attuned, coordinated and graceful dancing that is firmly grounded, flexibly resilient and fluidly moving far beyond their mastery of technical skills, competencies and proficiencies.

Being a relatively 'thin' presence and intuitively allowing and following the vital Ch'i energies of Spirit wherever and however they are moving and playing about in and through the open spaces, e.g., pauses, rests, intervals, gaps and silences, between the solid ego-structures, defenses and resistances and ongoing interactions of human beings, and are thus experiencing a frictionless, effortless and seamless attending relationship/process that is not energy depleting and/or exhausting.

Working with difficulties in the attending relationship/process by not resisting, opposing or forcing them but by attending closely, concentrating fully and proceeding slowly and carefully until, often quite suddenly, they simply and naturally come apart, drop off and fall away.

3-3 ❖ Heaven-Given Spirit

Text

A wayfarer startled by the sight of man with only one foot exclaims, 'What is this! How did you lose a foot? Is is the workings of Heaven or human beings?' The man explains, 'It is the working of Heaven that gives life, determines appearance and has destined me to be a one-footed human being.

The marsh pheasant may have a difficult walk of some distance for a single beakful of food or water, but, even so, it does not want to be kept and fed in a cage. Though it might even be treated royally, its Spirit would be broken.'

COMMENTARY

True attenders are:

Accepting that the gifts, talents and genius of their Virtuosity/Te; as well as their limitations, deficiencies and inadequacies, are endowments (en-Tao-ments) of Heavenly Tao that constitute their absolutely unique individual nature, form, integrity, character, power and efficacy.

Appreciating and opting for the wholeness, intactness and integrity of their Human Spirit and its freedom from the confining limitations of collective consciousness, social conditioning, conventional behaviors and the domestication of its inherent Tao-nature/Virtuosity/Te, even when its nourishing beneficence may be difficult and/or delayed.

3-4 ❖ Not Hiding from Heavenly Tao

TEXT

Lao Tzu dies, a wayfarer goes to the funeral site, cries out three times and quickly leaves. A disciple catches up with her asking, 'Are you a friend of the Tao-Master?' 'Yes', she replies. The disciple continues inquiring, 'Is the way you mourned him proper?'

The wayfarer explains, 'I regarded Lao Tzu as a True Tao-Master until I arrived here and saw the old and the young wailing as if they had lost a child or parent. He must have done something unnatural to have gathered such an emotionally attached following. This is forgetting the Heaven-given Source and natural state of life, getting lost in sentimentality and hiding from Heavenly Tao.

The Tao-Master came because it was his time and he left because he followed along with the natural flowing and completing of life which is beyond joy or sorrow and is being freed from the bonds. The firewood of life is consumed but the fire-flaming of Spirit burns on and no one knows where or when it will end.'

Commentary

True attenders are:

Being true to their innate Tao-nature/Virtuosity/Te, are remembering that Heavenly Tao is the real and true Source of the attending relationship/process and are not creating or fostering dependent attachments or addictive followings among human beings.

Experiencing that the true attending relationship meeting is a synchronistic event, a meaningful co-incidence and conjunction, happening along the Tao pathways of living because it is its time and is one that will naturally terminate because its life flows along.

Experiencing that the life and the terminating of a real, true, deep and full attending relationship are complete and beyond joy and sorrow and are understanding that, even though the attending relationship ends, their life goes on as does their Spirit, the Spirit of human beings and the Spirit of their working together.

TAO

Road/way/path
Speak/lead/guide
Principle/doctrine
Reality/Logos/Truth
Law/order/method
The Way

CHU
住

Reside/dwell in
Be/exist in
Live/live in
Stop/halt/stay
Completed action

CHU
居

Reside/dwell in
Be/present in
Live/life course
Stop/stay/remain
Occupy/inhabit

CH'U
處

Dwell/abide in
Rest in/occupy a place
Place/situation
Circumstance/condition
Manage/maintain

Opening the way to experiencing the constant unity of One/Complete Tao by:

Optimizing and elevating object-'others' *as* the intimacy/identity of relational unitive co-existing. Not separating, isolating, alienating, dividing, fragmenting, constraining, constricting and restricting experiential phenomena.

Stepping in and being with experiential phenomena just *as* they are being without externalizing, distancing and negating them.
Freely joining, connecting with, affiliating with, sharing with, identifying with, reuniting and residing with them.

In addition to engaging in the meditative practices of heart-mind fasting, sitting in oblivion and Origin wandering; Tao-Masters/Tao Chu, residing in/*as* Tao, are stopping, resting and remaining in place and are in charge of sustaining, transmitting and bringing the illuminating Light of Tao into human being, existing, living and experiencing.

RECORD FOUR
Being Human Amid Worldly Affairs

JEN

Human Being
Person/people
Humankind

CHIEN

Space between
Amid/among
In/internal

SHIH

Affair/event
Thing/matter
Business/undertaking

RECORD FOUR
Being Human Amid Worldly Affairs

Central Themes

The fourth Record of the *Nei P'ien* is about fluidity, fasting, openness, following along, not overdoing and uselessness.

True human beings are certain of identifying *as* Tao, are stabilizing their vital energies/Ch'i and are embodying the inner truth of their Virtuosity/Te before trying to 'use' Tao for any reason or purpose. In doing so, they are realizing that Tao is a pure unity, emptiness and wholeness that successfully completes activities when not mixed or filled with anything like intentions, motives, purposes, policies, plans or strategies to change or to improve human beings or affairs.

True human beings are preserving the integrity of their Virtuosity/Te by not seeking name, fame or gain or by using learning to conflict and to contend. They are understanding the unique dispositions, inclinations and tendencies of the individual natures of human beings and are relating to them free of careless needs and overdone actions to advise, influence, reform, convert or 'help' them.

True human beings give up such motivations through heart-mind fasting which involves clearing, emptying and stilling their ego-minds, hearts and wills of concepts, desires and impulses and opening themselves up to Tao and Spirit-Sourced activity. They are experiencing that essential, necessary and appropriate activity naturally flow from this inner state of openness and 'listening' with Ch'i/vital energy.

True human beings are forgetting ego, are obeying Tao and its operations and are serving Higher Mind with the same sense of fate and duty that children have for parents and subjects have for rulers. They are identifying with the unity, sincerity, simplicity and amicability of the beginning of affairs. True human beings are being honest, truthful, genuine and authentic in their interpersonal relationships and communications without using clever words, devising cunning schemes or taking crafty actions. They are not overdoing, exceeding the limits of situations or forcing the completion of events in human and worldly affairs.

True human beings are nourishing and not displaying their innermost, deepest, centermost, truest and utmost Tao-nature/Virtuosity/Te; are letting their minds move freely and are going along with things in the ways that they are going. They are flexibly and fluidly following along with activities and are allowing human beings to develop according to their own natures and destinies without being drawn out of their own integrity. True human beings are understanding and not going against the unique inner nature of individual beings and are not overvaluing or overestimating their own talents and abilities to affect and influence them.

True human beings are respecting the Sacredness of the sheer and utter being and presence of human beings and the efficacious power of their Virtuosity/Te. They are preserving the sanctity, vitality and longevity of being and living without evaluating or judging them by conventional standards of worthiness and usefulness.

True human beings may be appearing to be useless in terms of customary views but they are experiencing this apparent uselessness as very valuable and useful. By being identified *as* the empty and formless reality of Tao, concealing their Virtuosity/Te and appearing useless; they are escaping suffering the inevitable harm and injuries that often accompany ordinary useful worldly identities and activities and are thus preserving and extending their lives.

4-1 ❖ INTERNALIZING TAO

TEXT

A disciple is saying farewell to Confucius who asks, 'Where are you going? What will you be doing?' The disciple answers, 'I am going to a state where the ruler is immature, impulsive and irresponsible. He neglects the state and ignores his errors. The dead are lying everywhere and people have no refuge. You instruct us to leave a well-governed state to assist disorderd ones because 'Many ill people wait at the physician's door'. I want to use your instruction to remedy the situation.'

Confucius cautions, 'Ah! If you go there, you are risking your own life. Tao must be pure. When something is mixed in with it, there is confusion, busyness, trouble and failure. True human beings realize Tao in themselves before offering it to others. If you are not sure that you have it in you, you will not change this tyrant.'

COMMENTARY

True attenders are:

Like their professional colleagues who have interests in assisting human beings in maturing, regulating, understanding and developing themselves for their benefit and that of the human beings with whom they are associated.

Understanding that the effectiveness of the attending relationship/process is only as good as their own degree or extent of self-development and inner Tao-realization.

Affirming that their interest in assisting human beings is free of ego-centric motivations and self-interest, e.g., not being invested in and/or attached to being a 'do-gooder' or rescuer whose purposeful interferences and interventions may be risky and may only create confusion and difficulty and result in failure.

4-2 ❖ Virtuosity and Fame

Text

Confucius continues, 'Virtuosity is destroyed by fame and learning is used for contending. Fame causes people to fight each other and learning is the weapon. Both can be destructive instruments rather than means for completion.

You seem to be virtuous, faithful, trustworthy and non-competetive. But if you do not undertand people's nature, minds and Spirit and lecture this tyrant on correct behavior, you are only plaguing him by using his failures to demonstrate your superiority and you will be plagued in turn.

If the tyrant likes good people and dislikes bad people, there is no need to reform him. If he does not, you would be better off keeping your 'do-gooder' advice to yourself, otherwise he will probably try to defeat you. You will become dazed, apologetic and acquiescent. This is like trying to put out fire with fire or adding water to a flood and will only make matters worse. If you start out by giving in, there will be no end to your concessions.

On the contrary, if you speak out forcefully against the tyrant, he will not listen and will probably have you put to death. In ancient times, several well-meaning officials offended their rulers by trying to comfort the common people and were executed for using their Virtuosity for fame. Even True human beings have difficulty dealing with tyrants, so how could you not? But did you have some plan or way of proceeding in mind?'

Commentary

True attenders are:
Not misusing their Virtuosity/Te by using their knowledge of theories and techniques to compete or contend with human beings and are not seeking name, status, fame, gain or ego-gratification in their work.

Understanding that the goodness, kindness, faithfulness, trustworthiness and effectiveness of their Virtuosity/Te need to be complemented and supported by an understanding of human nature and the predispositions, sensitivities, vulnerabilities and 'psychologies' of human beings.

Not oppressing human beings by lecturing, giving advice and being either overly compliant and 'helpful' or overly assertive and confrontive; which are objectifying, distancing and alienating them and only escalating matters and creating defensiveness, resistance, power struggles and transference acting-out that are the result of empathic failings that risk and usually result in termination of the attending relationship/process.

4-3 ❖ PLANS AND STRATEGIES

TEXT

The disciple responds, 'I will be honest, confident, wholehearted and persevering. That should do.' Confucius exclaims, 'What! How can that work? You may put on a brave front but your inner uncertainty will show through. Tyrants relish in dominating others and exploiting their feelings. If he is not living ordinary virtues, how do you expect him to appreciate higher ones? He will be obstinate, self-validating and unbending without any change of heart. How can you succeed in this way?'

The disciple adds, 'Well, then I will be inwardly upright, outwardly respectful and use examples from antiquity. Inwardly, I will follow Heaven, knowing that the ruler and I are both sons of Heaven. Outwardly, I will follow the customs of people by acting courteously and deferentially. Regarding antiquity, I will follow ancient tradition, speak the words of sages and will not be superior, dishonoring or blameworthy. Would not that work?'

Confucius again counters, 'No, no, no! How can that work? You have too many concepts, plans and strategies and are not seeing what is needed. These preconceived ideas would probably keep you out of trouble but that is as far as they go. You are still trying to convert this tyrant by using your own concepts, plans and strategies. How can you possibly influence him?' The disciple allows, 'That is all that I can think of. What should I do?'

Commentary

True attenders are:

Experiencing that a professional persona of confidence, knowledgeability and authoritativeness and a professional demeanor of straightforwardness, wholeheartedness and perseverance are not necessarily effective in the attending relationship/process, especially if they are inauthentic compensations for inner feelings of insecurity or means of implementing treatment agendas.

Also experiencing that inwardly identifying and empathizing with human beings, outwardly acting respectfully and courteously and displaying the historical wisdom of traditional schools of psychotherapy/counseling are also not necessarily effective, especially if they are inauthentic motives, behaviors and promotions for outer indications of rapport.

Experiencing that motivated, premeditated and preconceived treatment plans and intervention strategies to effectively implement agendas, execute programs and achieve results are often obscuring what is really and truly needed for the attending relationship/process to be relevant, meaningful, useful and beneficial.

4-4 ❖ Heart-Mind Fasting

Text

Confucius indicates, 'You must fast.' The disciple queries, 'I have not eaten meat nor drank wine for many months. Is that fasting?' Confucius replies, 'No. I mean fasting of the heart-mind'. The disciple asks for clarification. Confucius continues, 'Your will must be One. Do not listen with ears but with mind. No...not with mind but with Ch'i, your vital Spirit-energy. Ears can only hear and mind can only think, but vital Spirit-energy is empty and open to receive and to respond to everything. Tao alone resides in this emptiness and openness which is the fasting of the heart-mind.'

The disciple allows, 'Before hearing this, I was certain of my identity but now I am no longer conscious of being a self. Is this emptiness?' Confucius assents, 'Yes, that is it! Let me explain. You can enter this tyrant's playpen but do not put yourself forward or be intrusive. If he listens, speak. If not, be silent. Do not have any opening and you will not be harmed. Always be at one and empty and accept whatever happens. Nothing else will do. Then you are close to succeeding.

It is easy to stop walking but hard to walk without making footprints. It is easy to trick people but hard to fool Heaven. It is easy to fly with wings but hard to fly without them. It is easy to act from knowledge but hard to act from non-knowing. Dwell in that empty inner centerspace, that sealed room where light is born. Fortune and blessing gather where there is stillness. Lack of stillness is running around while sitting down.

If you are inwardly open to everything you see and hear without concepts, plans or strategies; even gods and divine spirits will come to you, not to mention people. This is the way of transforming the myriad beings and things, the Pivotal Axis of Tao and the constant and secret practice of ancient sage-rulers. It is even more beneficial for ordinary people.'

Commentary

True attenders are:

Experiencing that the real preconditions and true preparation for effectively working with human beings in the attending relationship/process are fasting of the heart-mind, i.e., not attaching to sensory perceptions and mental conceptions and listening and attending with a clear mind, empty heart, still will and open Spirit.

Free of concepts, plans and strategies; are unified and identified with the mental clearness, emotional emptiness, volitional stillness and relational oneness of Tao and are open to receiving, reflecting, responding to and residing with anything and everything that human beings in the attending relationship/process are presencing.

Remaining at the Pivotal Axis and in the empty and open center of their Heart-Mind where the Pure and Clear Light of Tao is born and abiding and are accessing the intuitive sensing, awakened consciousness, inner visioning and divine intelligence of their Virtuosity/Te that are powerful transformative influences (in-flowings) for human beings.

4-5 ❖ Fate and Duty

Text

A minister who is being sent on an important mission to a neighboring state is consulting with Confucius prior to leaving. 'The state will probably be treating me with great respect but will be slow to start discussing. Ordinary people are not hurried much less a feudal ruler. I am very worried.

You say, 'In all matters, great or small, few succeed without following Tao. If unsuccessful, you will be criticized by others and, if successful, you will be imbalancing Yin/Yang. Only a True human being is not concerned with results or affected by outcomes.' I do not eat spicy foods or need cooling drinks but after receiving these orders, I am drinking pitchers of ice water! I am so anxious and feverish. I am already suffering Yin/Yang imbalance. This is beyond my capacity as minister!'

Confucius replies, 'In affairs of the world, there are two universal principles of devotion and loyalty that cannot be avoided.....fate and duty. It is fate to honor parents and duty to serve rulers and to do anything for them and to go anywhere with them. And to serve one's own Heart-Mind, unmoved by sadness or joy, accepting whatever happens and being content with the inevitable, is true Virtuosity. Being a son or a subject, there is always something unavoidable to do. In this case, do what has to be done, act truthfully and forget about yourself, loving life or fearing death and all should go well.'

Commentary

True attenders are:

Not experiencing anticipatory anxiety, fears of failing or being criticized and attachments to outcomes in conducting the attending relationship/process.

Trusting in their identifying *as* Tao as the true Source, context and agency of the attending relationship/process that is regulating its proceeding and bringing it to successful completion.

Devoted to and serving in their professional calling as a true attender, are honoring of and loyal to the human beings with whom they are engaged and, with true Virtuosity/Te, are contentedly accepting the inevitabilities of the attending relationship/process, are forgetting themselves and self-interest and are truthfully being however they essentially need to be and appropriately doing whatever they necessarily need to do.

4-6 ❖ Words and Trust

Text

Confucius continues, 'Let me tell you something else. If two states are close neighbors, their mutual trust is developed by trustworthy relations and actions. If they are far apart, their good faith is demonstrated through truthful messages. But conveying positive or negative messages between two parties is difficult to do. There is bound to be some untrue exaggeration of compliments or criticisms. Without truth, there is mistrust and messengers are endangered. So, speak the truth, do not exaggerate and you probably will not be harmed. Moreover, contests and celebrations usually all start out orderly and in good spirits but, when prolonged, often end up in anger and trickery and recklessness and chaos. So it goes with many things. They begin sincerely and simply and become deceitful and complicated if they go on too long.

Words are easily moved like wind and waves. One-sided monologues, half truths, clever words, unilateral actions, hidden agendas and crafty confrontations create anger and reactivity. Animals facing danger and death naturally growl ferociously and then attack. People threatened or pushed too far, automatically resent it and strike out. So, do not deviate from your instructions, exaggerate your words or press for completion. Do not force matters or exceed limits. Good completions take time and bad ones cannot be undone. You cannot be too careful.

So, flow along with whatever is happening, let your mind be free, nourish your inner being, stay content and accept whatever cannot be avoided. This is the ultimate. How else could you fulfill and complete your mission? Let everything work naturally, as difficult as that might be.'

Commentary

True attenders are:

Establishing and maintaining therapeutic alliances and collaborative attending relationships with human beings based upon good faith, clear agreements and communications, truthful dialogues and trustworthy behaviors.

Not forcing confrontations, pushing limits, manipulating interactions or accelerating premature closures with human beings engaged in the attending relationship/process that only create and result in defensiveness, resistance, reactivity, power struggles and transferential acting-out.

Being careful in conducting the attending relationship/process and are closely attending to and monitoring and according with and following its natural unfolding, proceeding, developing and completing while remaining centered in the Heart of Tao and their innermost, deepest, centermost, truest and utmost Tao-nature/Virtuosity/Te.

4-7 ❖ FOLLOWING AND HARMONIZING

TEXT

A tutor is assigned to a ruler and is consulting a minister/advisor about her concerns. 'This ruler is undisciplined, violent and the state is in danger. If I dare try to correct him, I will be in danger too. He sees faults in others but not in himself. What should I do?'

The advisor replies, 'Good question! Be careful and make certain you are acting appropriately. Be flexible while staying centered and maintaining the constancy and harmony of your Virtuosity without openly displaying it and risking being criticized, judged and overthrown. Outwardly follow along and inwardly harmonize with him but do not be drawn out and pulled into his doings. If he is acting childish, strangely or even reckless; be a little childish, strange and reckless with him. Then you can understand and connect with him and guide him back to his senses.

Do not be like the praying mantis that has such an inflated opinion of its own power that it tries to stop an oncoming carriage by standing in front of it waving its arms. Be watchful and careful and do not parade your talents or you will offend the ruler and court disaster. Be like the tiger trainers who do not feed live or whole animals to the tigers so as not to arouse their killing instincts and ferocious behavior. They know when the tigers are hungry and full and understand and follow along with and not go against their nature. Tigers can be trained and guided to be gentle by not stimulating their fierce natures and risking being killed. Some horse keepers are another example. They love their horses so much that they catch their urine and manure in shells and baskets. But if they brush flies off too quickly, the horses are startled and accidently kick them. The keepers are well-meaning but overdo their affections. Understand and respect the ruler's nature and do not try to be helpful.'

Commentary

True attenders are:

Staying grounded and centered in the efficacious power of their inner Tao-nature/Virtuosity/Te while understanding, empathizing, connecting with and following the natural dispositions and behaviors of human beings with whom they are meeting without becoming overly identified or enmeshed with them.

Not overestimating or displaying their talents and abilities; are respecting and understanding the ego-needs, protective defenses, survival mechanisms and coping strategies of human beings with whom they are meeting and are not threatening or violating their ego-structure and ego-integrity.

Appropriately timing reflections, interpretations, feedback, interactions, responses and interventions; are not playing into or colluding with the power struggles of aggressive human beings and are not advising, overdoing caregiving or invested in 'helping'.

4-8 ❖ Usefulness of Uselessness ❖ 1

Text

A master carpenter and his apprentice, on their way to a neighboring state, are noticing a Sacred tree growing at a village shrine. The tree is one-hundred spans around and so large that it can shade hundreds of oxen. It towers above surrounding hilltops and its lowest branches are eighty feet above ground and large enough to use for making boats. Crowds of people are gathered around the tree; the carpenter walks right by it but his apprentice stops and takes a long look at it.

Catching up with the carpenter, the apprentice asks, 'Since apprenticing with you, I have never seen such magnificent timber yet you walk right by it. How come?' The carpenter replies, 'Please say no more! The tree is useless. Boats made out of it will sink, coffins will rot, vessels will break, beams will split and doors will ooze sap. It is worthless and useless as a timber tree. That is why it has reached such a large size and an old age.'

After the carpenter returns home and retires, the Sacred tree appears to him in a dream saying, 'What are you comparing me with? Other useful fruit trees? Their worth is their undoing. After their fruit is picked, their branches are cut off and their Heaven-given lives are shortened because of their usefulness. I, on the other limb, have long been trying to be useless and have evaded destruction many times. Finally, I am useless and that is very useful to me. If I had been useful, could I have lived so long and grown so large? Besides, you and I are both things. How can one thing judge another thing? What does a useful dying person like you know about a useless living tree like me?'

The carpenter is sharing the dream with his apprentice who asks, 'If the tree has such desires to be useless, why is it serving as part of the shrine?' The carpenter retorts, 'Stop asking about the tree! The tree is just growing there in order not to be hurt by those who do not know that it is trying to be useless. If it did not become part of the shrine, it would have been cut down long ago. It is protecting itself in a different way from ordinary things. We are missing the point if we try to judge the tree in conventional ways.'

COMMENTARY

True attenders are:

Often not outwardly appearing to be relevant or useful to ego-identified colleagues who are practicing, or to human beings who are considering, conventional psychotherapy/counseling; in order to protect and to preserve the Sacredness, integrity and longevity of their innermost, deepest, centermost, truest and utmost Tao-nature/Virtuosity/Te.

Not interested in establishing yet another school of psychotherapy/counseling that is temporarily useful but relatively short-lived because of becoming a popular and passing fad that is abandoned after its utility, productivity and marketability are over.

Gratefully experiencing the sheer and utter reality and

actuality of the shared being and presencing of human beings living and growing together at the Sacred shrine of Life beyond any considerations, questions or judgments about relative worthiness and usefulness or worthlessness and uselessness.

4-9 ❖ Usefulness of Uselessness ❖ 2

Text

A wayfarer wandering in hill country is noticing a huge extraordinary tree able to shade hundreds of horse teams. 'What kind of tree is this? It must be very special wood.' But upon closer look, the wayfarer is noticing that the great trunk is too knotted and the large branches are too gnarled to be used for boats, coffins or rafters. He sniffs and tastes a leaf and it burns his mouth and intoxicates his brain. 'This tree is useless and good for nothing. No wonder it grew so large. Ah hah! This is the kind of uselessness that Holy human beings make good use of.'

Smaller trees are cut down and cut up in their prime for coffins, beams and monkey perches and never attain long life and full development. Such are the hazards of being useful. Similarly, oxen with white foreheads, pigs with upturned snouts and people with piles cannot be offered to the river gods because they would bring bad fortune. But for these reasons, Holy human beings consider them highly fortunate.

Commentary

True attenders are:

Again experiencing the Virtuosity/Te, Sacredness and the protecting and preserving usefulness of appearing irrelevant and useless to colleagues practicing and human beings seeking psychotherapy/counseling who are ego-identified and conventionally-oriented.

Not cutting up the original nondual Unity and Primordial Simplicity of Tao and the identity and integrity of their

Virtuosity/Te by making typically useful dualistic subject-object distinctions, analytic discriminations, conceptual dichotomies and theoretical formulations.

Seeming to be the original be-all and end-all 'good-for-nothings' of the traditional and conventional psychotherapy/counseling profession.

4-10 ❖ Usefulness of Uselessness ❖ 3

Text

Here is this severely hunchbacked human being; his chin resting on his navel, his shoulders rising up over his head and his neckbone pointing skyward. His vital organs are upside down and his hips are level with his ribs. He makes enough to feed and support himself and ten others by laundering and sewing clothes and by winnowing and sifting grain.

When other men are being conscripted for military service or being assigned to public projects, he is passed over for being a chronic invalid. When supplies are being handed out for the ill and disabled, he receives generous amounts of grain and firewood. If human beings whose bodies are so crippled can take care of themselves and others and live out their Heaven-given years, how much more is it possible for people with crippled Virtuosity!

Commentary

True attenders are:

Appreciating the silver linings of dark clouds and the disguised blessings in the lives of human beings suffering the crippling and disabling effects of trauma; physical, sexual and emotional abuse; violence and wounding.

Appreciating the resilient capacities and abilities of those victims and survivors who are able to access and actualize the inner strengths that enable them to courageously make the best of their conditions and to live reasonably meaningful and fulfilling lives.

Appreciating the Spiritual development of many victims and survivors as evidenced in their compassion, wisdom, acceptance of life and forgiveness of human beings.

4-11 ❖ Usefulness of Uselessness ❖ 4

Text

A madman is standing in front of Confucius's gate crying out, 'Oh Phoenix, Oh Phoenix. How Virtuosity has deteriorated. We cannot learn from past ages nor rely upon future ones. When Tao is present in the world, sages thrive. When Tao is absent, sages only survive. In times like the present, the best that can be done is to keep safe and stay out of trouble. Happiness is light as a feather but no one can lift it. Tragedy is as heavy as a boulder but no one can drop it.

Enough of oppressing people with teachings about Virtuosity! Stop overstepping their limits and setting them up for failure. Thorns thorns! Do not block my way. My path winds around you and you do not wound my feet. Just be empty and hide your light.

Mountain trees deplete themselves. Useful trees are felled. Torch oil consumes itself. Useful grease is burned. Everyone in the world knows about the usefulness of the useful, but no one understands the usefulness of the useless.'

Commentary

True attenders are:

Experiencing that when they are aligned with, attuned to and accorded with Tao and their Tao-nature/Virtuosity/Te; human beings are happily thriving, uplifted and enjoying life and when they are not allowing, following and complying with Tao; human beings are tragically surviving, downcast and only escaping harm.

Not oppressing human beings in the attending relationship/

process by lecturing about Tao, Virtuosity/Te and other difficult to attain ideals that may be beyond their limits to successfully reach and that consequently generate feelings of inadequacy, failure and insufficiency.

Being mentally, emotionally and volitionally empty; are openly facilitating and not hindering the full awareness or blocking the full actualizing of the unique talents, gifts and genius of human beings and their Virtuosity/Te; and are not using themselves up or burning themselves out in seemingly useful policies, purposes, plans and procedures.

HSING 性

Heart at birth
Inborn nature
Character/temperment
Natural disposition
Inclination of heart
Spirit

HUA 化

Change/convert
Transform/transmute
Smelt/melt
Dissolve/evaporate
Digest/influence
Yin/Yang Changes

Our inborn Tao-nature as human beings and the natural inclinations of our Hearts and Spirit are to be continually growing, changing and alchemically transforming.

RECORD FIVE
Virtuosity Fulfilling Agreement

TE

VIRTUE/MORAL EXCELLENCE
POWER/ENERGY/EFFICACY
CHARACTER/INTEGRITY
GOODNESS/KINDNESS

CH'UNG

FILL UP/FULFILL
SATISFY/SATIATE
SUFFICIENT/COMPLETE

FU

符

TWO HALVES OF A TALLY
MATCH/AGREE WITH
VERIFY/FULFILL
TALISMAN/CHARM

RECORD FIVE

Virtuosity Fulfilling Agreement

Central Themes

The fifth Record of the *Nei P'ien* is about Virtuosity, integrity, potency, efficacy, formlessness and wholeness.

True human beings are establishing perfect inner harmony which entails forgetting the form of the physical body and things of the external world; disallowing harmful desires, attachments, judgments and preferences and abandoning conventional social status distinctions and role hierarchies. They are, further, not seeking fame or reputation and are understanding and following their destiny.

Examples of the goodness of natural Virtuosity/Te are ordinary human beings who are not outwardly appearing to be physically whole, socially successful, psychologically developed or Spiritually evolved but whose Virtuosity/Te is formless, true, complete and trustworthy far beyond their seemingly deficient external appearances.

True human beings are identifying *as* Original Tao, are unifying all beings as One and are living beyond dualistic distinctions such as true-false, good-bad, right-wrong, likes-dislikes, gain-loss, Heaven-Earth and life-death. Their minds are one with Constant Mind and play in the freedom and harmony of Virtuosity/Te. The stillness, emptiness and clearness of their mirror-like minds positively reflect, influence and benefit human beings who are magnetically attracted and drawn to them.

True human beings are experiencing that Heaven is covering and sheltering and Earth is bearing up and supporting everything equally, that the precious Treasury of Heavenly Tao gives everything its unique existence and individual forms and that Tao is the foundation of human courage. They are nourished by Heavenly Tao and perfect and complete their corresponding Heavenly Tao-natures.

True human beings are remaining still and constant amid, and are freely unaffected by and living beyond, the shifting alternations of the world; are content with the workings of fate and destiny and are not letting them damage, displace or destroy their well-being, inner animating Spirit and Virtuosity/Te.

True human beings are peacefully according with Nature, letting everything be the way that it is and to transform in the way that it does and are not trying to change things or to help life along. They are not wasting the outflowing vital energy/Ch'i of their Virtuosity/Te and the precious gift of human life by intellectualizing and quibbling about the analytic distinctions and linguistic forms of discursive reasoning and syllogistic logic.

5-1 ❖ Constancy and Unity

Text

Here is a one-footed man who has as many followers as Confucius. A disciple is asking Confucius, 'This man is crippled yet he has as many followers as you do. He stands up but does not discourse and he sits down but does not discuss. People go to him empty and leave full. Is there a formless and wordless teaching? What kind of a person is he?'

Confucius answers, 'This man is a True Sage. I have been wanting to see him myself as should disciples and everyone else.' The disciple continues, 'He must be quite extraordinary. What is unique about the way he uses his mind?' Confucius replies, 'Living and dying do not affect him. Heaven-Earth could collapse but it would not move him. He clearly sees the true reality of things and is not influenced by external appearances. He holds fast to Tao and lets things be themselves and to change naturally.

We see things in terms of their differences. He sees all things as One, is not distracted by the senses, follows the natural equality and harmony of Virtuosity and is not troubled by loss. To him, losing a foot is like discarding a lump of earth.' The disciple asks, 'This man cultivates and perfects his mind but why do so many people gather around him?' Confucius answers, 'People see themselves reflected in still water rather than in running water. Only that which is still can still others.

Of things receiving life from Earth, pine and cypress are outstanding because their branches are constantly remaining green throughout the seasons. Of beings receiving life from Heaven, certain rulers are outstanding because their Virtuosity is constantly benefiting others throughout the state. Constantly holding fast to Tao is the foundation of courage. One courageous soldier may defeat a whole army even when only seeking fame.

But how much more can be done by one who governs Heaven-Earth, embraces the myriad things, is not attached to body and senses, unifies knowledge and has no concept of death. Such a human being chooses when to leave this world and to ascend to another dimension. People may become followers but he is not concerned with worldly affairs.'

Commentary

True attenders are:

Identifying *as* Tao and their Tao-nature/Virtuosity/Te and are experiencing that the true nature, real efficacy and courageous conduct of the attending relationship/process is in the power of their Tao-identified presence and not necessarily in forms and appearances, words and teachings and methods and techniques.

Tao-identified; are accepting and allowing of, unattached to and unmoved by, the natural vicissitudes, myriad fluctuations and various transformings of living and dying and are remaining grounded and centered in the original primordial and nondual Unity, Constancy, Equality, Harmony, Tranquility and Totality of Tao.

Unifying their Heavenly-Earthly natures, ordinary knowledge and universal Truth and the unique individualities and bipolar interrelationships of the myriad phenomena of the attending relationship/process and are not overtly interested in, nor concerned with, having a following of students, trainees or devotees.

5-2 ❖ Virtuosity and Destiny

Text

A wayfarer whose foot was amputated as a punishment and a Prime Minister are both students of a Master Teacher. At one point in a meeting, the Prime Minister says to the wayfarer, 'When we leave, I will go first and you will follow after me.' At the close of the meeting, the Prime Minister inquires, 'I am about to leave. Are you going to follow behind or not? When you see a Prime Minister, you do not even move out of the way. Do you think that you are my equal?'

The wayfarer replies, 'In our Master's house, is there such a thing as a Prime Minister? You are obviously proud of being one and being ahead of everyone else. I have heard that if a mirror is bright, dust and dirt do not settle on it. If they do, then it is not really bright. If one remains with a Master Teacher long enough, one will be without faults. Now, you regard our Teacher as a great Master and yet you talk and act like this. Is it proper?'

The Prime Minister retorts, 'Take a look at yourself. You seem to think that you are as good as an emperor. Examine your Virtuosity and you may have cause to reflect!' The wayfarer states, 'Many people justify their faults to avoid punishment but only a few do not excuse them and refuse to be forgiven. Only those with Virtuosity can accept the inevitable as their destiny. People wandering in front of an archer's target may get hit. If they do not, it is destiny.

There are many people with two feet who laugh at me for having only one. I used to get angry but after being with the Master, I am not troubled at all. Either he has purified me or I have come to my own acceptance. We have been Spiritual friends for nineteen years and he has never once acted as if my missing foot mattered.

Now, you and I are supposed to be wandering inwardly beyond the realm of outer bodily forms and social status and yet you pay attention to mine and external matters like who leaves first or last'. The Prime Minister squirms around, looks disconcerted and says, 'Say no more about it!'

Commentary

True attenders are:

Not concerned with differences in outer appearances, status and roles in relation to human beings and are phenomenologically and spatially being below, behind and inside of them rather than above, ahead or outside of them.

Free of the conceptual distinctions of psychotherapist/counselor and patient/counselee and are embodying the clarity of a mirror-like mind that seeks nothing, reflects everything and retains nothing.

Non-judgmentally accepting any unavoidable inevitabilities in the conducting of the attending relationship/process and are taking full responsibility and accountability for any empathic failures, procedural errors or derailing behaviors without excusing, rationalizing or justifying them.

5-3 ❖ Virtuosity and Heaven ❖ 1

Text

A man with no toes is hobbling in to see Confucius who says to him, 'You were careless, committed a crime and brought this punishment upon yourself. What is the use of coming to see me now?' The man replies, 'I did not know how to behave properly, took my body lightly and lost my toes. But now I am coming here seeking to preserve something far greater and far more precious than toes. There is nothing that Earth does not support and Heaven does not cover. I thought that you, a Master-Sage, would be like Heaven-Earth and not receive me in this way.'

Confucius apologizes and invites the man in to talk but he declines and hobbles away. Confucius then speaks to his disciples, 'This is a good lesson. A toeless crippled man is still willing to atone for and to learn from his past misdeeds. How much moreso should those who have not been as unfortunate.'

The man goes to see Lao Tzu and relates his experience saying, 'Confucius is not yet a perfected human being. He is only imitating one and trying to gain a reputation by pretending to know and to teach how we all should live. He does not know that True Sages consider such fame to be cuffs and fetters!'

Lao Tzu suggests, 'Why do not you just help him to see that life and death, acceptable and unacceptable are strung on the same single thread and free him from the cuffs and fetters?' The man replies, 'If Heaven is punishing him, how can he be set free?'

Commentary

True attenders are:

Experiencing that Heavenly Tao and Earthly Tao cover and protect and support and bear up human beings and are the real and true context and frame and ground and locus of the attending relationship/process.

Not negatively judging the past histories and behaviors of; and not marginalizing, pathologizing and criminalizing; unfortunate human beings and are taking seriously their at-one-ment and conversion to a deeper, higher and fuller Spiritual awakening, realization, development and evolution.

Avoiding being limited and bound by seeking a famous professional reputation, starting a school of psychotherapy/counseling or developing a following of devoted apprentices.

5-4 ❖ Virtuosity and Spirit ❖ 1

Text

A ruler is relating to Confucius, 'I knew of an ugly looking man who is gathering quite a following. Men regard him highly and women want to be his concubine rather than another man's wife. He never tries to lead or to pursuade people and always agrees with and goes along with them. He is not in a ruling or wealthy position to protect and provide for others. He only knows about what happens locally where he lives.

Moreover, he is so ugly looking that he could scare everyone under Heaven. Yet, people continually seek his company. There is something extraordinary about him, so I invite him over for a personal meeting. Indeed, he is ugly looking! I convince him to stay for awhile. I begin to see that there is something to him and, after a year, trust him completely. I offer him a position as Prime Minister but he is reluctant to accept and appears like he wants to refuse. Soon after that, he leaves. I am sad to lose such a person with whom to share the joys of the state. What kind of a person is he?'

Confucius answers, 'Once I am on a mission and see some piglets trying to nurse on their dead mother. After awhile, they abruptly leave her. What they needed and loved in her is not her body but the Spirit that animates it. A dead soldier has no need for medals and a footless man has no need for shoes. The basic foundation has been lost. Concubines do not pierce their ears or cut their nails. Newly wedded men avoid official positions involving dangerous missions. Such is the importance of keeping the body alive and whole. How much more important is it to preserve the integrity of Spirit and Virtuosity.'

COMMENTARY

True attenders are:

Magnetically attracting human beings who are typically disregarding their external physical appearance and are resonating with the radiant energy and vibrant potency of their Tao-nature/Virtuosity/Te.

Not leading, directing or pursuading human beings but, rather, are accepting, attuning to, according with and following along with them and are being trusted by them.

Purely and simply enjoying sheer and utter experiences of

being and living naturally and unofficially in the Tao-state, being together with human beings in attending relationships and identifying *as* the wholeness of vital energies/Ch'i, bodily integrity and the animating Spirit of Tao.

5-5 ❖ VIRTUOSITY AND WHOLENESS

TEXT

Confucius continues, 'Now this outwardly ugly looking man says, does and achieves nothing yet is loved and trusted. So you offer him an official high-ranking position and are only afraid that he will not accept it. It seems to me that his Virtuosity is whole and formless.'

The ruler then asks, 'What do you mean that his Virtuosity is whole?'. Confucius answers, 'Cold and heat, hunger and thirst, value and worthlessness, success and failure, profit and loss, wealth and poverty and life and death are all natural alternations in the order of things, the workings of fate. They continually trade places like night and day and no one knows where one begins and the other ends.

As such, they need not disturb our Harmony or displace our Spirit. Live so that you are constantly in harmony with the changes, intermingling with everything, delighting in making everything be Spring in your Heart and creating the moment... this is the wholeness of Virtuosity.'

COMMENTARY

True attenders are:

Being whole in their Virtuosity/Te by unifying and harmonizing the myriad bipolar Yin/Yang Ch'i phenomena of human existence and experience that are constantly, continuously and continually alternating, reciprocating and reversing in the attending relationship/process.

Not disturbing or disrupting their harmony or displacing and eclipsing their Spirit by investing in, attaching to or overidentifying with the inevitably transient changings of experiential phenomena and the workings of fate.

Accepting, intermingling with and delighting in all of the rich and varied experiential phenomena occurring in the attending relationship/process and are making everything be Spring in their Heart-of-Hearts, even experiences that are considered to be negative, errors, mis-takes, failures, etc.

5-6 ❖ Virtuosity and Formlessness

Text

The ruler continues asking, 'And what do you mean that Virtuosity is formless?'. Confucius answers, 'Balance is a perfect state like still water and can be taken as a model. It safeguards what is quiet deep inside and shows no outer surface movement. Virtuosity is a state of perfect Harmony, has no form and is not displayed yet nothing can escape its in-fluence (in-flowing).'

Later on, the ruler is sharing his experience with a disciple of Confucius. 'When I first faced South and became a ruler, I thought that doing my best is keeping people alive and the state in good order. But now, after hearing the words of Confucius, I fear that I had been misunderstanding what being a good ruler is. I ignored my own Spiritual development, squandered my vital energy and neglected the state. Confucius and I are no longer subject and ruler but are Spiritual friends and companions in Virtuosity.'

Commentary

True attenders are:

Not displaying the deep and full harmony of their Virtuosity/Te in any outward form yet are experiencing its efficacious power, transforming influence and harmonizing effect in the attending relationship/process.

Experiencing that the perfect balancing of Yin Ch'i/Yang Ch'i energies is the formless and undifferentiated Plenum Void/

Wu Chi at its maximum potential for manifesting form and that this deep inner state of emptiness, stillness and clearness is an 'absent presence' that human beings naturally fill with the vivid forms and moving activities of their beings and doings.

Relating to human beings engaged in the attending relationship/process as Spiritual wayfaring companions free of the traditionally ascribed and conventionally circumscribed subject-object and self-other identity and role distinctions and power differentials of so-called patient/counselee and psychotherapist/counselor.

5-7 ❖ Virtuosity and Forgetting

Text

Two rulers are closely associating with two wayfaring companions, one hunchbacked and club-footed and the other hunchbacked and goiter-necked. The rulers are so delighted with their two friends and their conversing that they regard the backs and feet of other human beings as too straight and their necks as too thin. When the goodness of Virtuosity is radiantly shining forth, outward appearances are forgotten. But when human beings do not forget what can be forgotten and forget what cannot be forgotten...this is indeed true forgetting.

Commentary

True attenders are:

Not judgmentally or preferentially concerned with the nature and form of the external appearances of human beings engaged in the attending relationship/process.

Experiencing that the goodness of their Virtuosity/Te and the radiance of their energy/Ch'i alone are the powers of Presence that are an activating, potentiating, transforming and harmonizing in-fluence (in-flowing) in the attending relationship/process.

Experiencing that the efficacious energy and potency of their radiant presence are naturally accompanied by not forgetting the myriad seemingly extraneous and irrelevant phenomena of the attending relationship/process and also by forgetting even Tao and the Virtuosity/Te of their Tao-nature.

5-8 ❖ Virtuosity and Heaven ❖ 2

Text

True and free human beings have their wanderings and wonderings and let everything pass through their consciousness. To them, conventions are sticky glue, morality is a patch-job, learning is a by-product and skills are goods-peddling.

Since they do not make distinctions, they do not need gluing with conventions. Since they do not lack anything, they do not need fixing with morality. Since they do not make plans, they do not need operating with learning . And since they do not sell goods, they do not need promoting with skills. These four are the sufficiently nourishing and ultimately sustaining food of Heaven and supercede needing or requiring things from people.

True and free human beings have the form and appearance of other human beings but not their dualistic desires, judgments, preferences, investments, attachments and sentiments. So, they can live together in the human world but are not affected by its rights and wrongs. Small, they enjoy their human nature together. Great, they complete their Heavenly Tao-nature alone.

Commentary

True attenders are:
Wandering and wondering in the attending relationship/process and are allowing all of its myriad experiential phenomena to pass through their conscious awareness without defining, distorting, deviating nor directing them.

Not only concerned with:
1. The being of things and the making of pathological

diagnostic distinctions and have little need for clinical assessments.
2. The knowing of objects and the making of conceptual case formulations and have little need for theoretical objectifications.
3. The doing of actions and the making of strategic treatment plans and have little need for technical methodologies.
4. The having of results and the making of prognostic outcome claims and have little need for promotional skills.

Obtaining their nourishing, sustaining and fulfilling blessings, gifts and graces from Heavenly Tao and are completing their extraordinary Heavenly Tao-nature while enjoying their ordinary human nature but are not using the attending relationship/process for ego-gratification, self-satisfaction or personal gain.

5-9 ❖ Virtuosity and Spirit ❖ 2

Text

The logician Hui Tzu is asking Chuang Tzu, 'Can human beings really be without feelings?' Chuang Tzu answers, 'Yes, we can.' 'But', continues HuiTzu, 'If human beings do not have feelings, how can you call them human beings?' Chuang Tzu replies, 'Heavenly Tao gives us our body, form and appearance. Why should not we be called human beings?' Hui Tzu persists, 'But if they are already called human beings, how can they be without feelings?'

Chuang Tzu continues, 'That is not what I mean by feelings. I mean that we do not let likes and dislikes disturb or harm our inner Spiritual well-being. We let things be as they are and not try to change or improve them or to help life along.' Hui Tzu then asks, 'If human beings do not try to help life along, how do they survive?'.

Chuang Tzu then reiterates and adds some cogent and trenchant observations, 'Heavenly Tao gives us our bodily form and appearance. We do not disturb or harm our inner Spiritual well-being with likes and dislikes. Now, you are treating your Spirit like a stranger. You are wasting your vital Spiritual energy on external things. You are leaning against this tree muttering and quibbling, slumping down on this rotten tree stump and starting to fall asleep. Your human body is Heavenly Tao's precious gift and you are misusing it to logically gibber-jabber about conceptual attributes like hardness and whiteness.'

COMMENTARY

True attenders are:

Understanding, appreciating and sharing their Heavenly Tao-given incarnation with human beings engaged in the attending relationship/process and are accepting them as they are being and appearing even when some of their characteristics and behaviors could be seen as logically inconsistent with being human beings.

Fully identified with the essential nature and existential qualities of human being but are not allowing emotional investments in, and attachments to, dualistic distinctions, judgments and preferences to affect the integrity and vitality of their Tao-nature/Virtuosity/Te or to use them to attempt to change, improve or help along the life of the attending relationship/process.

Not being concerned with conceptual distinctions, discursive reasoning, syllogistic logic and intellectualized debates with human beings engaged in the attending relationship/process and are not indulging in analytic and logic-bound semantic hair-splitting, pointless nit-picking, fruitless quibbling and Spirit-enervating, wearying and exhausting inquiry into, and rhetorical discourse about, the nature of concepts like 'normal' and 'chronic'.

CHEN	JEN

REAL/TRUE	'MAN'/PERSON
GENUINE/AUTHENTIC	HUMAN BEING
SPIRITUAL/DIVINE	HUMANKIND
NATURAL STATE	EVERYONE
UNFEIGNED	POPULACE
THOROUGHLY	MASSES

TRUE/SPIRITUAL HUMAN BEINGS WHO ARE THOROUGHLY GENUINE/STRAIGHTFORWARDLY VISIONING/NATURALLY TRANSFORMING FROM AN ELEVATED FOUNDATION.

THEY ARE CHARACTERIZED BY:
UNCONVENTIONALITY
CLARITY/RELATIVITY
EQUALITY/VACUITY
FLUIDITY/TRANQUILITY
INTERCHANGING/TRANSFORMING
FREEDOM/SPONTANEITY
DESTINY/INEVITABILITY
TRANSCENDING/IDENTITY
BEING-TAO

RECORD SIX
Great Kindred Teacher

TA

Great/big/large
Vast/extensive
Noble/high ranking

TSUNG

Ancestral/kindred
Great master
Honor/venerate

SHIH

Teacher/instructor
Master/leader
Sage/expert

RECORD SIX
Great Kindred Teacher

Central Themes

The sixth Record of the *Nei P'ien* is about trueness, impartiality, transforming, transmitting, forgetting and identifying.

True human beings are understanding the difference between the Tao of Heaven and the Tao of Human Being and that Heavenly Tao is the harmonious integration and cooperation of Human Tao and Earthly Tao.[11] They are using knowledge to reach ultimate non-knowing and are understanding that true knowledge is not absolute or certain and that it is not always clear which is Heavenly Tao or Human Tao. True knowledge first depends upon True human beings.

True human beings are mild, calm and carefree; constant, deep and clear and moderate, tolerant and hesitant. They are not resisting need, priding in plenty, planning affairs, regretting errors or displaying successes. True human beings are beyond dualities such as liking or disliking things, loving life or hating death, preferring being or non-being and caring about succeeding or failing and profit or loss. They are enjoying the endless transformings of human beings, are going along with what is right for others, are enriching all without partiality or attachment, are doing whatever needs to be done and are not being opportunistic or exploitive.

True human beings breathe deeply up from the heels; do not savor their food; are stable, secure and sufficient; are empty and know their limits; are reasonable, correct and timely in their activities; do not use their minds to repel Tao or try to use what is human to assist what is Heavenly. They are good, wise, talented and free and immune to external influences, harm and injury.

The understanding of True human beings is advanced and reaches all the way to Tao. They are understanding that Heavenly

Tao gives everything their life, form, growth and death and are constantly aware of Heavenly Tao's presence and operating in the world, Nature and the universe. True human beings are loving Heavenly Tao as their parent and ruler, are willing to die for the Truth of Tao and have realized and are One with the Heart of Tao. Their bounty enriches and transforms human beings and they are residing and resting in and modeling the Original Spirit and Virtuosity/Te of Tao.

True human beings are forgetting appearances, distinctions, externals, attainments, conventions and ceremonies. They are content with the times, are not bound by and are going along with things, are forgetting about and not disturbing changes, are accepting and allowing being transformed without knowing the 'whys' of changing and are cycling in life without beginning or ending. True human beings are integrating all forms of human being and are wandering free and easy in non-doing and the *as*-isness of everything.

True human beings are simplifying living, are companions of both Heavenly Tao and human beings, are one with Tao, are thriving and forgetting themselves in Tao and are wandering beyond the world. They are not dreaming when asleep nor troubled when awake. True human beings have awakened from the dream of being an 'I' living a life and are one with the Mystery, Miracles, Marvels and Magnificence of the Reality and Truth of Tao.

Tao is formless but real, unborn and undying, yet is originating, transforming, completing, dissolving and returning everything. It is prior to and endowing (en-Tao-ing) everything with its absolutely unique individual nature and identity; both terrestrial, natural, human and mortal and celestial, supernatural, divine and immortal. Tao covers Heaven and bears up Earth and is deeper than the deepest, higher than the highest and older than the oldest.

True human beings are opening to Tao by sitting-forgetting body, senses and mind; preferences, likes and dislikes and benevolence, righteousness and propriety; which are leading to their transformation and becoming identical to Tao. Tao can be transmitted to and attained by talented human beings through a sequential process of studying texts, oral teachings, clear understanding, according and unifying, realizing potentiality, wondrous expression, experiencing dark obscurity and Mystery, empty Void and, finally, identifying *as* Non-Beginning and the Source (Tao). Tao can be transmitted by Tao-identified human beings to other talented human beings who are able to detach themselves from; and to transcend the limitations of; world, things, self, life, time and death and to attain illumination, identity *as* Tao and its infinity, eternity and immortality.

True human beings are singular human beings, unified, merged and identified *as* Heavenly-Earthly Tao; are being Tao-like, are impartially supporting and covering human beings and are passing on the gift of life to them. They are accepting the alternatings and transformings of Great Yin and Great Yang; the destiny of the human life course and the inevitability of birthing, growing, declining and dying. For True human beings, being and non-being, existing and non-existing and living and dying are One and dying is a natural passing on, a freeing of the bound and a transformative transitioning and returning that is accepted without sorrow or grief.

True human beings are freely wandering with Tao, Heaven-Earth, Nature and Spirit as Teacher and Guide, in the realm beyond the world of dust and dirt where all are preserved; are ascending to and roaming within the infinite Heavenly mists and are entering the Mysterious Origin and Oneness of Heavenly Tao.

6-1 ❖ True Human Being

Text

True human beings are understanding what comes from Heaven and are attuned to and accorded with it. They are understanding what comes from human being and are using their knowledge of the known to develop an understanding of the unknown and are living out their Heaven-given years in the culmination of knowledge. But there is a consideration. Knowledge is based upon something but what that something is, is not certain. How do we know that what we experience as Heaven is not really human being and vice versa? Before there can be true knowledge, there must be True human beings.

Commentary

True attenders are:

Clearly distinguishing what comes from either Heaven or human being, are according with their Heavenly Tao-nature/Virtuosity/Te and are using their knowledge of what is known about the attending relationship/process to develop an understanding of the unknown Mystery of Tao and the Tao-nature/Virtuosity/Te of individual human beings.

Realizing that understanding is based upon uncertainty and are experiencing the bipolar Yin/Yang Ch'i interchangeability and paradoxical realities of experiential phenomena occurring in the attending relationship/process.

Experiencing that a true understanding of human beings is based upon and following from the degree, extent and level of development of their own true human being.

6-2 ❖ Breath and Life

Text

Who are True human beings? The True human beings of old accept neediness, do not pride in abundance, do not make plans and do not regret errors or display successes. They do not fear heights, are not soaked by water nor burned by fire and attain Tao.

True human beings of old sleep without dreaming, wake without cares, eat without savoring and breath deeply from their heels, unlike common people who; caught in limits, passions and desires; gasp for air. They do not love life nor hate death, do not delight in coming nor grieve at going, do not forget the beginning nor seek the ending and simply accept and enjoy receiving and returning. True human beings do not use their minds to resist Tao or to assist Heaven. Such are True human beings.

Commentary

True attenders are:

Experiencing that their true understanding of human beings is directly corresponding with, and proportionate to, the depth and fullness of their being true attenders.

Understanding that some of the constituents of being true attenders are not using esoteric theoretical concepts, not making elegant treatment plans, not resisting Spiritually transformative energies, not priding in effective interventions, not regretting technical errors, not displaying successful results and not avoiding financial shortfalls.

Meeting challenges without fear, are working with deep and intense emotions without being adversely affected, are drawing energetic support from the Earth and their belly center and are grateful for the opportunity to participate in the attending relationship/process for as long as it lasts, remembering its beginning, not seeking its ending, accepting and enjoying its mutuality and reciprocity and not grieving its termination.

6-3 ❖ Self and Others

Text

True human beings are having empty minds, calm faces and unfurrowed brows. They are cool as Autumn and mild as Spring; their joy and anger flow like the seasons; they are in harmony with all things and have no limitations. True human beings never lose the hearts of people, even when waging war and defeating nations. Their blessings shower the myriad beings equally, impartially and nonpersonally.

True human beings are not delighting in success, not showing partiality, not being opportunistic, not seeking fame or gain or not being untrue to themselves. Many leaders have lost their lives by trying to reform others, by displaying their Virtuosity, by doing the bidding of others, by neglecting their own best interests and by finding no joy in their lives.

Commentary

True attenders are:

Being clear, crisp, calm and mild; are flowing freely with their feelings; are in harmony with human beings and are not experiencing limitations in the attending relationship/process.

Impartially beneficent and compassionate toward human beings even during conflicts and power struggles and are not being omniscient, opportunistic or seeking name, fame and gain in the attending relationship/process.

Not being untrue to themselves, are not displaying the Virtuosity/Te of their gifts and talents, are not trying to change human beings or necessarily complying with their wants and are experiencing enjoyment in the life and work of the attending relationship/process just for what and *as* it is.

6-4 ❖ Integrity and Light

Text

True human beings of old are grounded, upright, straightforward and steadfast. They are humble but not servile, correct but not demanding and vast but not lofty. True human beings are relaxed, cheerful, transparent and tolerant; radiate inner light and reside and rest in their Virtosity/Te. They are part of the world yet stay inner-directed and centered in the midst of others, are beyond being influenced and are seemingly oblivious to their surroundings.

True human beings consider laws and ceremony to be the body and wings of government, knowledge and reason to be a requirement and guide and are structured, responsible, lenient and inspiring. They act imperatively and effortlessly yet people think that they are trying hard.[14]

Commentary

True attenders are:

Grounded, solid, upright, straightforward, centered, relaxed, transparent and vast in their interactions and interventions with human beings.

Independent, inner-directed, humble, tolerant, receptive and responsive but not overly compliant or affected and influenced by the changing needs of human beings or the ongoing requirements of the attending relationship/process.

Embodying their Virtuosity/Te and radiating its Inner Light, are conducting the attending relationship/process consciously, rationally, appropriately, responsibly, ethically and accountably and are inspiring and uplifting to human beings.

6-5 ❖ Heaven's Tao

Text

True human beings are unifying Non-Being and Being, unity and disunity, Heaven and human being and likes and dislikes. They are understanding that life and death are the inevitable nature of things, destined by Heaven. True human beings are regarding Heaven as a parent to live for and a ruler as a superior to die for and, even moreso, to live and die for Tao and Truth. When Heaven and human being are unified, integrated, harmonized and co-operating; there is a True human being.

When springs dry up and fish are stranded on dry ground, they try to wet each other by spewing but this is no substitute for forgetting themselves in rivers and lakes. When people are praising or blaming rulers and others, it is more beneficial if they forget them and immerse themselves in Tao.

COMMENTARY

True attenders are:

Unifying Non-Being and Being, Heaven and human being, living and dying and likes and dislikes while working with these and other bipolarities in the experiences of human beings.

Accepting the inevitabilities and transience of Heavenly Tao's workings, the existential facticity of human beings' living and dying and the initiating, finite life and terminating of the attending relationship/process.

Regarding, honoring and complying with the Reality and Truth of Heavenly Tao as a loving parent and sovereign ruler; are not praising or blaming colleagues or human beings; are unifying, integrating and harmonizing their Heavenly Tao-nature and human nature and are forgetting themselves in Tao.

6-6 ❖ EARTH'S TAO

TEXT

True human beings are understanding that Earth limits us with a body, works us with life, eases us in old age and rests us in death and that the Tao that makes our lives good is also the same Tao that makes our deaths good.

A boat hidden in a ravine or a fishnet sunk in a lake may seem safe from theft but in the middle of the night someone may steal them unbeknownst to their sleeping owners. People do not understand that no matter how well small things are hidden within larger ones, they can still be lost. But if the world is hidden inside of the world, then there is no way to lose it. This is the Ultimate Reality of the Constancy of things.

COMMENTARY

True attenders are:

Understanding that Earthly Tao is limiting human beings with a body, working them in life, easing them in old age and resting them in death which is the same life cycle of the course of the attending relationship/process in its phases of initiation, duration and termination.

Experiencing that the nonpersonal and impartial beneficence of Earthly Tao make life good and also make death good, beyond the differing conceptions, valuations and attachments made by human beings.

Not seeing untended psychological entities like body, ego, mind and personality as smaller and lesser ones that can; during the slumbering of life; be safely and well hidden within larger and more awakened and highly valued and cultivated psycho-spiritual entities like Spirit, Self, Psyche and Soul but, rather, are seeing them as mutually corresponding and equally valuable ones in their own right, in the Ultimate Reality, Nondual Integrity and Complete Constancy of their unique identity and inner Tao-nature/Virtuosity/Te as human beings.

6-7 ❖ Manifestations of Tao

Text

We are born in human form and find joy in our mortal physical body and its myriad finite transformings. True human beings are wandering among those things that can never be lost and, so, live forever. They are delighting in both the beginning and the ending of life, whether it is long or short, and are being examples and models for everyone. How much more should we emulate Tao, that which originates and completes all beings and upon which the great transformations of living depend.

Tao has Reality, Truth and indications but no form or actions. It can be transmitted and received by Heart but is invisible and intangible. Tao is its own Root-Source, exists before Heaven-Earth and gives Spirit to goddesses and gods. It is above the zenith and below the nadir, but is not high or low; before the most ancient and earliest, but is not old.

When attaining Tao:
   Heaven and Earth harmonize   Immortals descend
   Sun and moon shine   Emperors govern
   Constellations course   Sages enlighten
   Divine beings incarnate   Human beings thrive

COMMENTARY

True attenders are:

Enjoying their human incarnation and its constant, continuous and continual transformings and those of human beings engaged in the attending relationship/process.

Identifying *as* Infinite-Eternal Tao; are willingly accepting and modeling the flowing transiency of human life and the attending relationship/process and are experiencing ancient Tao as the invisible, formless, intangible and actionless ultimate Ground and Source of all of its experiential phenomena and their transformings.

Realizing that attaining Tao; like all cosmic, divine, immortal, mythical, sovereign, Sacred and human beings that do; is reaching the conclusion, completion, consummation and culmination of their real inner nature and true inner identity.

6-8 ❖ TRANSMITTING TAO

TEXT

A wayfarer is meeting a hunchbacked woman and asks, 'You are old yet look like a young girl. How come?' The woman replies, 'I have found Tao.' The wayfarer then asks, 'Can Tao be learned?' She answers, 'Oh no! How could that be? Besides, you are not the one to do it. Some people have the talent of a sage but not the Tao of a sage. I have the Tao of a sage but not the talent.

Once, I try to teach a fellow with the talent of a sage but it is not easy and takes quite a long time. He first is able to transcend the physical world, material things and people and, after some time, is able to transcend all life. He slowly begins to achieve clear vision and to see the Oneness of Tao everywhere and in everything. And some time after that, he begins to transcend past, present and future and the life that birthing does not begin and dying does not end. He is able to welcome and affirm everything, reject or negate nothing and to attain and maintain complete peace in the midst of conflict and struggle. This is what completely identifying *as* Tao is.'

The wayfarer then asks, 'How do you learn all of this?' And the woman replies, 'I learn it through studied writings, repeated recitations, clear insights, full attunements, realized experiences, witnessed Miracles, Dark Mystery, Empty Void, No-Beginning and Living Tao.'[15]

Commentary

True attenders are:

Experiencing that it is possible for professional colleagues and human beings engaged in the attending relationship/process to educate and cultivate the natural gifts, talents and genius of their innate Tao-nature/Virtuosity/Te and to progressively realize Tao, if and when that is their interest, talent and ability.

Experiencing that, through their awakened and attentive teaching, training, supervising, consulting and mentoring; the traditional contents, focuses, processes and conducting of conventional psychotherapy/counseling practice can be transformed and transcended and a way opened to envision, embody, relate and enact what true psychotherapeutic attending really is.

Able to understand, experience and identify with Tao as the essentially timeless and Mysterious Origin and Completion of the attending relationship/process through studying Taoist texts such as Lao Tzu's *Tao Te Ching* and Chuang Tzu's *Nei P'ien,* memorizing passages and tales, understanding meanings, assimilating truths and directly realizing the Ultimate Reality, Constant Miracles, Dark Mystery, Empty Void and Sourceless Openness of Living Tao.

6-9 ❖ Transforming in Tao - 1

Text

Four Tao-Masters are discussing, 'Whoever believes that Nothingness is the head, life is the spine and death is the buttocks and experiences that they are all One shall be a friend.' They are looking at each other, smiling in complete agreement in their hearts and become close friends.

Shortly thereafter, one of the Tao-Master friends becomes gravely ill and is visited by another. The ill one says, 'Great is the Creatrix that I am this deformed. My spine is curved around, my organs are upside down, my chin rests on my navel, my shoulders are up over my head and my neckbone points to the sky. My reflection in the well water shows me what the Creatrix has created me as. The Yin/Yang is all jumbled up.' Yet he seems to be calm.

The visiting Tao-Master friend inquires, 'Are you not upset?' and is answered, 'Oh no, why should I be? If my left arm becomes a rooster, I will declare the new dawn and if my right arm becomes a crossbow, I will have a gamebird for dinner. If my buttocks becomes wheels and my Spirit a horse, I will take a good ride. We are born because it is our time and we die according to the nature of the way things go. If we are content to accept and to follow along with whatever happens, joy and sorrow cannot affect us. This is freedom from limits and bondage and the way it has always been with Heaven. How can I be upset?'

Commentary

True attenders are:

Experiencing that being, existing and living and Non-Being, non-existing and dying are one unity that is the deep underlying reality and essential truth of the attending relationship/process and are accepting its myriad phenomena and transformings as they come and go, regardless of their forms.

Accepting and going along with the dynamic Yin/Yang Ch'i

changings and the kinetic Wu Wei Ch'i flowings in the attending relationship/process, are not upset by their natural restructuring and transmuting and unfolding and developing and are anticipating whatever new forms of phenomena, being, relationship and process are emerging.

Experiencing that the life of the attending relationship/process, like everything else, has its own time and duration and naturally passes on and are contentedly accepting its here-now moments; having freed themselves from the limiting and confining bondage to preferred physical appearances, mental concepts, emotional feelings, volitional activities and relational behaviors.

6-10 ❖ Transforming in Tao - 2

Text

Soon after, a second Tao-Master friend of the four becomes terminally ill and lays struggling with breathing while his family is gathered around him crying. Another Tao-Master friend comes to visit him and says to them, 'Quiet, give him some space and let the transformings happen.' Turning to his friend, he says, 'Great is the Creatrix. What will you be used for now? Where will you be sent? Will you be made into a rodent's innards or an insect's leg?'

The ill friend replies, 'A son goes wherever his parents tell him to, in any direction. Yin/Yang are the real parents, brought me to this state of dying and I am obeying them without blame. Great Earth gave me a body, worked me in life, eased me in old age and is resting me in death and that which has made my living good is also making my dying good.

If a skilled smith is casting metal and it suddenly jumps up and says, 'Only make me into a famous sword!', he certainly would take it as a bad omen. Now, when being cast in human form, if I had said to the Creatrix, 'Only make me into a famous man!', that too would be a bad omen. Heaven-Earth is a great melting crucible for transforming and the Creatrix is a skilled smith. Then what could happen that is not fitting? So, I calmly go to sleep and awaken freshly.'

COMMENTARY

True attenders are:

Stepping back, are making space for and are not interfering with the natural transformings of the attending relationship/process as it is originating, unfolding, proceeding, developing, progressing and completing without blame or regret.

Understanding that the life course of the attending relationship/process microcosmically corresponds with that of the human life cycle and its sequential developmental stages of birthing, growing, declining and terminating.

Not egocentrically, ignorantly and arrogantly insisting that whatever is naturally and spontaneously happening in the attending relationship/process should be any better or different than it is and are aligned with, attuned to and accorded with the goodness of its Heavenly-Earthly nature, creative transformings, calm endings and fresh beginnings.

6-11 ❖ FORGETTING IN TAO

TEXT

Three Tao-Masters are saying to each other, 'Who can be together without being together and cooperate without cooperating? Who can fly up to Heaven, wander through the mists and clouds, go beyond the limits of space-time and forget life forever?' They are looking at each other, smiling in complete agreement in their hearts and becoming close friends.

Shortly thereafter, one of the three dies. A disciple of Confucius is sent to the funeral service and finds the two other Tao-Master friends playing lutes and singing a song, 'Alas, alas, you have gone back to your true nature while we remain human beings.' The disciple asks them, 'Is it proper to be singing in the presence of a corpse?' The two friends look at each other, laugh and reply, 'What do you know about ceremony?'

The disciple returns to Confucius and recounts the event. 'What kind of people are they, so disregarding of protocol, behaving improperly, singing in front of the corpse with such irreverance?' Confucius apologizes, 'I should not have sent you to attend the funeral service. They travel beyond this physical world, we travel within it and the two will never meet. They are One with the Creatrix of things and the One Breath of Heaven-Earth.

They see life as a swelling tumor and death as a bursting boil and do not discriminate between life and death. They consider the body as an accidental arrangement of random parts and forget their organs and senses. They come and go, beginning and ending and beginning over and over again without limitations. Carefree, they wander beyond this dusty world, dwelling in Non-Being and non-doing. How can they be concerned with social conventions, ceremonies and appearances?'

The disciple asks, 'Why then are you, Master, concerned with them?' Confucius replies, 'I am mandated by Heaven to do so and you and I have this in common.' The disciple asks for clarification. 'Fish thrive in water and are nourished there. Human beings thrive in Tao, work without doing and actualize their nature. Fish need to forget themselves in lakes and rivers and human beings need to forget themselves in the arts and cultivating of Tao.'

'May I ask more about these two strange people?' Confucius finishes, 'They are only strange to human beings but very familiar to Heaven. The inferior person of Heaven is superior in the world of human being and the inferior person in the world of human being is the superior person of Heaven.'

Commentary

True attenders are:

Happily sharing the freedom of the true attending relationship/process; the Non-Being of Tao, the non-doing of Wu Wei Ch'i and the natural spontaneity of Tzu Jan and are freely wandering in the realms of non-ordinary consciousness beyond the space-time and life-death limitations of the human world.

Conducting the attending relationship/process within the physical world of ego-consciousness but are simultaneously identifying *as* the transphenomenal Reality, Unity and Identity of Original Tao and Heaven-Earth.

Thriving in Tao and being companions of Heaven who have forgotten most everything, themselves and even Tao, are not necessarily conducting the attending relationship/process according to conventional protocols and may be judged by some professional colleagues to be too radical and unprofessional.

6-12 ❖ SIMPLIFYING AND FORGETTING

TEXT

A disciple is asking Confucius about the behavior of a Tao-Master, 'When her mother dies, she does not cry nor appear sad at heart. How can she have such a good reputation?' Confucius answers, 'She has mastered Tao, gone beyond wisdom, simplified her life, does not know why we live or die or which comes first or last and accepts her present state of being without any concern for future transformations.

When we are changing, how do we know we are changing or whether we are not changing? How do we know if we have not already changed? Maybe you and I are still dreaming and have not woken up. The Tao-Master shares grieving but regards death as a change of abode and her Spiritual Harmony is not disturbed.

She is the only one who is awake. Moreover, we talk about an 'I'; I do this or that, but how do we know that such a thing even exists? We dream of being a bird flying through the high skies or a fish diving in the deep waters. But I do not know if we are still dreaming. Running around judging others is not as good as laughing and laughing is not as good as letting things take their natural course and going along with them. Be content to follow along with what is happening, forget the changes and enter the Mysterious Oneness of Heaven.'

COMMENTARY

True attenders are:

Identifying *as* Tao, are going beyond wisdom and are simplifying the attending relationship/process by only doing what is essential, necessary, appropriate, relevant, practical and useful without investment in results or attachment to outcomes.

Accepting the here-now realities, actualities and transformations of the attending relationship/process without necessarily being concerned about its future forms, changes, transformations and directions.

Awakened from the dream of being an ego-self, are letting the attending relationship/process take its natural course and following along with it, are energetically constant and Spiritually content in the face of terminations and are re-affirming and re-experiencing the Mysterious Oneness of Heavenly Tao in their work with human beings.

6-13 ❖ Forgetting and Wandering

Text

A recluse and a student are discussing his teacher. The recluse asks, 'So, what is he teaching you?' The student replies, 'He instructs me to practice benevolence and righteousness and to clearly distinguish between right and wrong.' The recluse responds, 'Then why are you coming to see me? He is already marking you with benevolence and righteousness and cutting off your nose with right and wrong. How do you expect to wander freely along any remote wilderness paths just doing what you like?'

The student replies, 'That may be but I would at least like to wander along the borders if possible.' The recluse says, 'Not possible. Blind people are not able to appreciate the beauty of people's faces or the colors of embroidered silks.' The student counters, 'But there are women, men and rulers who have forgotten their beauty, strength and wisdom; are purified and transformed by the Creatrix and have become disciples. Maybe this can happen for me.'

The recluse responds, 'Well, we cannot tell yet but let me give you a general outline. My teacher, my teacher. She harmonizes the myriad things and enlivens the myriad generations but is not considering herself benevolent or righteous. She is more ancient than the oldest antiquity but is not regarding herself as long-lived. She covers Heaven, bears up Earth and follows all beings but is not considering herself skilled. It is with her alone that I wander.'

Commentary

True attenders are:

Being assisting and appropriate in their attending relationship reflections, interpretations, interactions and interventions but are not attached to traditional and conventional notions of benevolently doing 'good' or righteously being 'right'.

Forgetting and transcending the limitations and blindness of their social conditioning, academic learning and professional training sufficiently enough to not allow them to interfere with their natural awakening, developing and transforming.

Freely wandering in the spacious, expansive and unlimited realms of non-ordinary and higher consciousness, are supporting and following human beings and are bringing their state of awakened consciousness into their professional work as true, vitalizing, harmonizing and transforming psychotherapeutic educators, trainers, supervisors and mentors.

6-14 ❖ Sitting Forgetting

Text

A disciple of Confucius is giving him a progress report. 'I am improving.' Confucius asks, 'What do you mean?' and the disciple relates, 'I have forgotten doing good and being right.'

Confucius says, 'Well, that is all right and good but not sufficient.'

Days later, the disciple meets again with Confucius reporting, 'I am improving' and Confucius asks, 'How so?'. The disciple answers, 'I have forgotten rites and music.' Confucius says, 'Well, that may be worth celebrating but it is still not sufficient.'

More days later, the disciple returns again saying, 'I have improved' and Confucius asks again, 'In what way?' The disciple states, 'I just sit and forget everything!'. Confucius looks surprised and asks, 'What do you mean by sitting and forgetting?'

The disciple explains, 'I am not physically attached to my body and form or mentally attached to knowing and understanding anything and I am completely identifying *as* Tao.' 'That is it!', exclaims Confucius. 'Identifying *as* Tao, you must be free of judgments and preferences and be constantly transforming. So, you are worthy enough to be followed!'

Commentary

True attenders are:

Progressively disidentifying from and forgetting ego-investments in, and attachments to, doing 'good' and being 'right' in the attending relationship/process.

Further disidentifying from and forgetting the absolute nature of the theoretical formulations and rules, interpersonal relationships and roles and methodological techniques and rites of their traditional and conventional psychotherapy/counseling education and training.

Finally forgetting and being liberated from objectifications of, and attachments to, physical body-based sensory preferences and mental mind-based conceptual judgments and are completely identified *as* Tao and its constant transformings.

6-15 ❖ Poverty and Destiny

Text

It has been raining for days and a Tao-Master decides to visit and check on a Tao-Master friend of hers and packs up some food, thinking that she may be having a difficult time. Arriving at the gate of her friend's hut, she hears lute playing and a faint lamenting refrain, 'Oh father, oh mother, is it Heaven, is it human being?'

The friend enters, bows, pauses and inquires, 'Why such a lament?' Her friend explains, 'I am wondering what has brought me to this extreme. I cannot understand it. My parents are not wanting me to be this poor. Is Heaven-Earth singling me out to be so poor? I cannot discover the cause. Yet, here I am in this wretched state. It must be destiny.'

Commentary

True attenders are:

Experiencing that it is often difficult to clearly discern and accurately determine the true source of the multi-determined presenting issues, psychological conditions, persistent symptoms and unwanted experiences of human beings.

Open to exploring personal histories and family of origin issues to discover possible etiological factors in the questions, problems, conflicts, difficulties, struggles and sufferings human beings bring to the attending relationship/process.

Also open to the possibility and reality that some of the issues that are focused on in the attending relationship/process are beyond identifiable cause-effect relationships at the level of psychological understanding and may be a matter of destiny, fate and fortune; the mysterious inevitable workings of Heavenly-Earthly Tao.

TZU	LE/LO

Self	Joy/rejoice
I/me/my	Happiness
Personal	Cheerfulness
Naturalness	Gladness
Spontaneity	Pleasure
Freedom	Laughter

The quintessential/existential/salvational experience of human being/being human is the Spiritual freedom/joyful happiness of being-Tao in the awakened consciousness/lives of true/genuine/authentic human beings.

RECORD SEVEN
APPROPRIATE ATTENDING AND REGULATING

YING

OUGHT/SHOULD/MUST/NECESSARY
RIGHT/PROPER/APPROPRIATE/SUITABLE/FITTING
RESPOND/REPLY/PROMISE/FULFILL
ACCEPT/AGREE TO/OBEY/COMPLY WITH

TI

帝

SUPREME RULER
EMPEROR/EMPERORSHIP
SOVEREIGN

WANG

KING/PRINCE/KINGSHIP
RULER/MONARCH
ROYAL/IMPERIAL[16]

RECORD SEVEN
Appropriate Attending and Regulating

Central Themes

The seventh Record of the *Nei P'ien* is about mirror-mind, heart center, spontaneity, totality, mastery and completion.

True human beings are being empty, open, peaceful and easy going. They are not holding personal views and are unconcerned with knowledge, plans, schemes, projects, merit, praise, promotion or fame. True human beings are beyond the worlds of both human and non-human and are identifying with all forms of being and life. They are not devising their own principles, standards, regulations and ceremonies; are safeguarding their inner Tao-nature, Self, Soul and Spirit and are not controlling, regulating or governing what is external to or outside of themselves.

True human beings are making sure of their identity *as* Tao before acting and; when their conscious awareness is empty, clear and open; appropriate actions naturally and spontaneously follow and flow from it without friction, effort or depletion. They are letting everything and everyone spontaneously find their own way in life according to their uniquely individual natures and abilities. Their activities and workings have far-reaching transformative influences but are appearing not to be of their own doing and are not depended upon or celebrated by human beings. True human beings are letting their minds wander in purity, simplicity and sufficiency; are blending their Spirit with the vastness of Tao and are harmoniously following along with the coursing of events, the inevitability of fate and destiny and the lives of everyone and everything just *as* they are being and going.

True human beings are identifying with the spontaneity of fathomless Tao and wandering in Nothingness and boundlessness beyond the limits of the ordinary physical and social worlds. They are keeping to and safeguarding the endowment (en-Tao-ment) of their Heavenly Tao-nature/Virtuosity/Te which is completely true, truly complete and trustworthy. True human beings are embodying the endless and wandering in the pathless. Their mirror-like minds are empty and clear; seeking nothing, receiving and reflecting everything and retaining nothing and they are considering everyone and everything as blessed gifts of Heavenly Tao.

True human beings have fully attained and realized Tao, are completely Tao-identified and have mastered the vital energies of their Yin/Yang Ch'i interchanging dynamics and Wu Wei Ch'i flowing kinetics. They have the ability to consciously access, change, regulate and transform inner energy states at will, yet do not have inflated or grandiose opinions about being able to create or influence the states and healings of human beings.

True human beings are fully, wholly and completely embodying/personifying the Primordial Unity and Simplicity of transcendent pre-differentiated Tao in the empty and open space of their Heart Center, the Pivotal Axis and Central Kingdom of Tao. They are welcoming the alternating, balancing, harmonizing, centralizing, voiding and reversing of Yin/Yang Ch'i vital energies without being affected by them.

True human beings are sustaining and maintaining the purity and integrity of their original undifferentiated and non-dual wholeness by not attaching to, investing and indulging in or identifying with sensory differentiations, perceptual distinctions and conceptual discriminations or logical and well-intentioned ideas, agendas, plans, strategies and programs to change, alter, revise and convert the way beings and things naturally are.

7-1 ❖ Perfect Virtuosity

Text

A disciple is questioning another disciple. He asks a question four times and each time receives no answer. He is delighted and rushes over to inform his Tao-Master who says, 'Are you just now learning that there are no answers to questions?

There are two rulers and one is no match for the other. The first ruler is benevolent and tries to win people over. He never leaves the world of 'human' to get into the realm of Non-Human. Now, the second ruler is still when she sleeps and empty when she awakens. Sometimes she takes on the Spirit of horses and oxes. Her Virtuosity is perfectly true and truly perfect. She is beyond distinctions of human and Non-Human.'

Commentary

True attenders are:

Delighted by/in non-knowing and questioning the answers, rather than answering the questions, of human beings engaged in the attending relationship/process.

Not invested in nor attached to doing 'good', not colluding with human beings to win them over and not making dualistic conceptual distinctions between psychotherapist/counselor and patient/counselee or between what is human being and what is non-human being.

Trusted by human beings because the Virtuosity of their inner Tao-nature is completely true and truly complete and because they are clear, still, empty and open and able to empathize and identify with the various forms of their being and experience.

7-2 ❖ Governing with Virtuosity

Text

A student runs into a madman who asks him, 'So, what does your teacher tell you?' The student replies, ' He tells me that a ruler should establish his own principles, standards, regulations and ceremonies so that everyone will obey them and be law-abiding subjects.' The madman counters, ' This is false Virtuosity! Governing the world in this way is like trying to wade across the ocean, dig up a river or make a mosquito carry a mountain.

When True human beings govern, they do not rule what is on the outside. They make sure of themselves first and then act. When their conscious awareness is clear and empty, necessary and appropriate actions naturally follow and flow from it and they just do what they can do or what needs to be done. That is all. Birds fly high in the sky above to avoid arrows and pellets and mice dig deep in the earth below to avoid smoke and shovels. Do you have any less sense than these creatures?'

Commentary

True attenders are:

Not subverting the Virtuosity/Te of their inner Tao-nature by idiosyncratically establishing ethical standards, regulating clinical practices and instituting formal rituals on their own and are necessarily and appropriately relegating such matters, structures and activities to professional administrators and licensing boards.

Experientially affirming their Virtuosity/Te and are focusing more upon the internal realities and inner truths of the experiences of human beings and less upon their external appearances and outward compliance.

Experiencing that necessary and appropriate interpretations, interactions and interventions naturally follow and flow from the clarity, depth, fullness and connectedness of their conscious awareness; are trusting in the autonomous self-regulating of human beings engaged in the attending relationship/process and are allowing, supporting, facilitating, guiding and following however and whatever they are essentially, reasonably, sensibly, necessarily and appropriately being and doing.

7-3 ❖ Governing the World

Text

A wayfarer wandering on the south side of a mountain encounters a Nameless sage and asks her, 'May I ask you how to govern the world?' She says, 'Oh, go away foolish man. What kind of idiotic question is that? I am about to join the Creatrix of everything. Soon I will ride the great bird of openness and easiness far out beyond the limits of the world and universe and freely wander in the land of No-thingness and Vastness. Please, do not bother me with questions about governing the world.'

But the wayfarer persists and the Nameless woman relents, 'Let your mind wander calmly and freely in purity and simplicity, let your Spirit be one with openness and vastness, allow and follow along harmoniously with the natural order and course of things and do not have personal attachments and judgments... then the world will be well governed.'

COMMENTARY

True attenders are:

Regulating the attending relationship/process by being Spiritually identified with the openness, spaciousness and vastness of Tao and by allowing their heart-minds to calmly and freely wander in the purity and simplicity of Tao without preconceptions and predispositions to know or to do anything.

Regulating the attending relationship/process by harmoniously allowing and following along with its natural coursing, unfolding, proceeding and developing without personal investments in, or attachments to, its directions, results and outcomes.

Experiencing that regulating the natural coursing, unfolding, proceeding and developing of the attending relationship/process can be interfering with openly and freely riding the energy of Tao out beyond the spatio-temporal limitations of ego-consciousness and wandering in the emptiness and limitlessness of deeper and higher extraordinary Consciousness.

7-4 ❖ ENLIGHTENED GOVERNING

TEXT

A student is consulting with Lao Tzu and asks, 'If people are alert, keen, strong and diligent in understanding and conducting things and in their studying of Tao and its operations, are they comparable to enlightened sage-rulers?' Lao Tzu answers, 'Compared to enlightend sage-rulers such people are like laboring servants and craftspersons bound up in their work, wearing out their bodies, depleting their energies and troubling their minds and hearts.

The markings of tigers call out hunters. The agility of monkeys and the abilities of dogs call out trainers. How could the people you describe be compared with enlightened sage-rulers?' The student is surprised and then asks, 'Well then, may I ask how enlightened sage-rulers govern?'

Lao Tzu assents, 'When enlightened sage-rulers govern, their accomplishments reach everyone but they do not appear to be doing anything. Their influence harmonizes and transforms everyone but they are not depended upon. They bring enjoyment to everyone but they are not celebrated. They are identified with the unfathomable and wander where there is nothing at all.'

COMMENTARY

True attenders are:

Often unlike many of their professional colleagues who are confident and persevering, have a thorough knowledge of specialized theories and techniques, are dedicated to the craft of psychotherapy/ counseling and spend considerable time, labor and energy advertising their services, networking for referrals, increasing clientele, developing their practices and being concerned about income.

Usually relatively unknown, and do not foster dependent attending relationships or take credit for successful accomplishments; yet the efficacious power, gifts and genius of their Virtuosity/Te are influential, harmonizing, transforming and uplifting to human beings.

Tao-focused and centered, Tao-embodied and personified and Tao-identified and Tao-like human beings who, while conducting and engaging in the outward practicing of the attending relationship/process, are inwardly solidly grounded and deeply centered in the emptiness, openness, spaciousness and vastness of Tao.

7-5 ❖ There is More to It

Text

Lieh Tzu is telling his Tao-Master about a local shaman, 'He tells anything about people, their gains and losses, fortunes and misfortunes. He predicts the length of their lives and divines the exact time of their death as if he is a god. People run away at the sight of him. I go to see him and am completely fascinated. I used to think that your Tao is perfect but now I see something even more perfect.'

The Tao-Master responds, 'So far I have only shown you the outer forms and not the inner Spirit of Tao. Do you believe that you have mastered Tao? If there is no rooster in a flock of hens, there are no fertile eggs or baby chicks. You use your limited understanding of Tao to make people believe in you but they can see right through you. Bring the shaman here and let us have a look at him.'

The next day, Lieh Tzu brings the shaman to meet the Tao-Master. After the meeting and as the shaman is leaving he says, 'I am very sorry to report that your Master is dying and will not last another week. I saw something very strange, like wet ashes.'

Lieh Tzu, soaked in tears, recounts this information to the Tao-Master who reassuringly says, 'Do not worry. Just now I showed the shaman the still pattern of Earth in the lower belly energy center, with nothing standing and nothing moving. I closed off and reserved my vital Ch'i energy. Bring the shaman back again.'

The following day, the two return again and this time after the meeting and as the shaman is leaving he says, 'It is fortunate that your Master met me. He is better already and going to live. I could see his vital energy stirring.' Lieh Tzu happily reports back to the Tao-Master who says, 'This time, I showed the shaman my vital Ch'i energy slowly rising up from Earth in the lower belly energy center and beginning to move, ascend and start to circulate. Now, bring the shaman back again.'

The following day, the two return again and after this meeting and as the shaman is leaving this time he says, 'Your Master is never the same. I cannot read him. When he stabilizes, I will return to re-examine him.' When Lieh Tzu reports this, the Tao-Master says, 'This time I showed the shaman the great alternating and reversing and circulating and returning Yin/Yang and Wu Wei Ch'i energies of Heaven-Earth that are balancing and transforming in the middle heart energy center. I was equalizing the stillness and swirling of Ch'i energies flowing in the vast abysses of empty space. Now, bring the shaman in yet again.'

The next day, when the two return, before they even sit down, the shaman runs out of the room. The Tao-Master says to Lieh Tzu, 'Go run after him and bring him back in.' But Lieh Tzu is unable to find him and returns asking about what had happened. The Tao-Master explains, 'This time I showed the shaman the undifferentiated No-thingness before the originating of things. I let the Primordial Ch'i energies spring up from the Void however they do from Heaven in the upper head energy center. That is why he ran away.'[17]

After this experience, Lieh Tzu realizes that he has not begun to understand very much about Tao, the efficacious power of its Virtuosity and the workings of its Ch'i energy. He goes home, does not go out, cooks for his wife, does domestic chores and feeds the animals. He forgets about worldly affairs, lives simply and simply lives. Grounded and centered in the Earth and his body and heart amid life's distractions; he remains One with Tao until the ending of his lifetime.

Commentary

True attenders are:

Not publically demonstrating the efficacious power of their Virtuosity/Te at professional conventions, weekend workshops or on celebrity talk shows and are progressively revealing the reality and depth of the principles, processes and potency of their attending relationship practices to committed students, supervisees, trainees and interns in appropriate circumstances and under appropriate conditions.

Experiencing that, while they may be achieving intuitive abilities and psychic powers as natural by-products and side-effects of their Spiritual developing; they are not ego-identifying with them and are not displaying and uncritically utilizing them to work with human beings or to egocentrically assume responsibility for 'reading' and healing them.

Sometimes, Spiritually developed enough to be able to exercise conscious control over the presence, balancing, circulating and transforming of their vital Ch'i energies in the three belly, heart and head energy centers/elixir fields/Tan T'ien of their physical body.

7-6 ❖ Guidelines for Governing

Text

Do not seek fame, make plans or become lost in knowings and doings. Internalize, assimilate, embody, personify, enact and identify *as* Tao and its dynamic-kinetic operations and wander in the vast spaciousness and limitlessness where there are no pathways. Become and be all that Heaven endows you with but do not think that you have received or attained anything. Be completely empty and open, that is all. The heart-mind of True human beings is like a clear mirror; seeking nothing, receiving and reflecting everything and retaining nothing. True human beings are allowing their activity to naturally and freely flow from their deep connection with Tao and the awakened consciousness and open awareness of their clear mind, empty heart, still will and One Spirit without contention, conflict, friction, effort or depletion.

COMMENTARY

True attenders are:

Not making fixed psychodiagnostic assessments, case formulations, treatment plans, intervention strategies or outcome prognoses; are not becoming and being lost in theoretical knowings and methodological doings and are not seeking fame or gain in their attending relationship practice.

Experiencing that all of the experiential phenomena of the attending relationship/process are manifestations of Tao and its dynamic-kinetic operations, are humbly and modestly identifying *as* Tao and their endowed (en-Tao-ed) Virtuosity/Te and are open to follow along with human beings and to freely wander along the unmapped wilderness frontiers and pathless paths of non-ordinary consciousness and the vast spaciousness and unlimitedness of Tao.

Embodying a mirror-like heart-mind that seeks nothing, receives and reflects everything and retains nothing; are remaining clear, empty, still, whole and open; are acting without contention, conflict, friction, effort or depletion and are being grateful for the endowed (en-Tao-ed) blessings of their innate Tao-nature/Virtuosity/Te bestowed upon them by Heavenly Tao.

7-7 ❖ UNDIFFERENTIATED BEING

TEXT

The ruler of the Southern Sea is Shu (sudden/abrupt/hasty/brief) and the ruler of the Northern Sea is Hu (sudden/unexpected/hasty/careless) and the ruler of the Central Region/Middle Kingdom is Hun Tun (Primordial Chaos/Undifferentiated Unity).

From time to time, the rulers of the Southern and Northern Seas regularly meet in the Central Region/Middle Kingdom of Hun Tun and are always welcomed and graciously received.

The two rulers are wanting to repay Hun Tun's kind generosity; agreeing and deciding that, 'All human beings have seven openings by which they breathe, see, hear and eat but Hun Tun has none. Let us give him those.'

So, every day for seven days, Shu and Hu, the rulers of the Southern and Northern Seas, make one opening in Hun Tun's whole body and, on the seventh day, Hun Tun dies.[18]

Commentary

True attenders are:

Experiencing that the Ruler of the Central Region/Middle Kingdom is the Undifferentiated Being and Unity and the Center of Human Being, the Pivotal Axis of Tao and their very own clear, empty, open and whole Heart Center and Heart-of-Hearts.

Experiencing that their Heart-Mind Center is the meeting place of the alternating, balancing, centralizing, voiding and reversing Yin Ch'i/Yang Ch'i vital energies that, when perfectly harmonized, are the undifferentiated plenum void state at its maximum potential for originating and manifesting all of the myriad diverse forms of the experiential phenomena occurring in the attending relationship/process.

Experiencing that interpretations, interactions and interventions that are opening up discrete sensory, perceptual and conceptual experiences can be destroying the Original Undifferentiated Unity, Identity, Primordial Simplicity and Totality of Tao and the wholeness, integrity, vitality, pure potentiality and efficacious potency of their inborn Tao-nature/innate Virtuosity/Te and its inherently unique gifts, talents and genius.

MING

DESTINY/FATE/INEVITABILITY
DECREE/COMMAND/ORDER
HEAVENLY DECREE/MANDATE
DIVINE COMMAND/GOD'S WILL
CELESTIAL GIFTS/APPROVAL
LIFE/LIFE SPAN/LIFE CALLING

CH'ENG

COMPLETE/WHOLE
FINISH/END
MATURE/FULLY DEVELOPED
ACCOMPLISH/SUCCEED
ATTAIN/BECOME
PERFECT

CH'UAN

COMPLETE/COMPLETION
FINISHED/ALL DONE
ENTIRE/TOTAL/ALL
ABSOLUTE
WHOLE/FULL
PERFECT

DESTINY AND FATE ARE NOT PREDETERMINED AND FATALISTIC REALITIES THAT IMPOSE LIMITATIONS ON THE FREEDOM AND POSSIBILITIES OF HUMAN BEINGS. IT IS AN INEVITABLE REALITY, HOWEVER, THAT ALL

HUMAN EXPERIENCES AND HUMAN LIFE ITSELF ARE FINITE AND TRANSIENT AND WILL, AT SOME POINT, REACH AN ENDING AND FINAL DESTINATION. BUT WITHIN THE LIFE OF HUMAN EXPERIENCES AND THE SPAN OF HUMAN LIFE, THERE ARE COUNTLESS OPPORTUNITIES FOR US TO MAKE CONSCIOUS CHOICES CONCERNING THEIR ACTUALITIES, CHARACTERISTICS, DIRECTIONS AND OUTCOMES.

THE END-POINT OF HUMAN BEING, EXISTING, LIVING AND EXPERIENCING IS THE CONCLUDING, COMPLETING, CONSUMMATING AND CULMINATING FINAL DESTINATION OF WHAT, HOPEFULLY, HAS BEEN A FULFILLING JOURNEY THAT HAS INCLUDED SOME OF THE SYNCHRONISTIC MEETINGS, SPONTANEOUS MOMENTS, SURPRISE DISCOVERIES, JOYFUL AWAKENINGS AND SERENDIPITOUS PERFECTION THAT OFTEN GO ALONG WITH A WAYFARING THAT HAS FOLLOWED THE CONTOURS, VALENCES, VECTORS AND TRAJECTORIES OF THE UNPLANNED ACTUALITIES OF HUMAN LIVING.

PARADOXICALLY, OUR HUMAN FREEDOM FOLLOWS FROM THE ACKNOWLEDGING, ACCEPTING AND ALLOWING OF; THE ADJUSTING, ACCOMODATING AND ADAPTING TO; THE ATTUNING TO, ALIGNING AND ACCORDING WITH AND THE ABIDING BY, IN AND *AS*, THE ABSOLUTE REALITIES, NECESSITIES AND LIMITATIONS OF THE UNIQUELY INDIVIDUAL CIRCUMSTANCES AND CONSCIOUSLY AWAKENED EXPERIENCES OF OUR LIVES.

Conclusion

Psychotherapeutic Commentaries

This rendition has included psychotherapeutic commentaries for tales within each of the seven *Interior Records*. Additional tales selected from the *Outer* and *Miscellaneous Records* and their commentaries are presented in Appendix One of the rendition. In Appendix Two are included succinct statements for each of the *Nei P'ien* tales that provide a quick reference to the essential message transmitted in each tale and/or its psychotherapeutic commentary.

The following is some general commentary on psychotherapy/counseling, patients/counselees and psychotherapists/counselors and some specific practical applications of the principal experiential concepts and psychotherapeutic commentaries to the attending relationship/process.

Psychotherapy/Counseling

The professional practice of individual psychotherapy/counseling is a human resource, activity, service and opportunity available to human beings who are in need of assistance in living their lives and being themselves. It is a professional fee-for-service interpersonal relationship and activity with a structure and requirements and expectations and anticipations for both the patients/counselees/clients and the psychotherapists/counselors/therapists engaged in it. In the psychotherapeutic commentaries of this rendition, so-called psychotherapy/counseling has been referred to as the attending relationship/process, so-called psychotherapists/counselors and so-called patients/counselees have respectively been referred to as wise attenders and human beings who are engaged in the attending relationship/process.

The attending relationship/process, in addition to being regulated by legal and ethical standards and practices, is grounded in the characteristics and qualities of any optimal and trustworthy human relationship or activity that values human nature, respects human dignity, recognizes human worth, honors human uniqueness, supports human being, assists human living, encourages human endeavors, facilitates human growth, guides human development and is of benefit to human beings by insuring their personal safety and preserving, sustaining and fostering their human rights to life, well-being, freedom and happiness.

The professional practice of both traditional and conventional and alternative, complementary and integrative psychotherapy/counseling now relates to and involves a wide range of human wisdom and activities in the fields of philosophy, religion, theology and Spirituality; the physical, medical, behavioral, social and human sciences and the liberal and fine arts; in so far as they are concerned with the understanding, developing, expressing, transforming, healing and evolving of human beings and human existence; as well as with conscious human living as a fundamentally and essentially Spiritual journeying of the Human Soul. It is noteworthy that the etymological meaning of the very word, 'psychotherapy' is 'attending the Soul'.

Humanistic, existential and transpersonal psychotherapeutic approaches do not minimize, contradict, negate or substitute anything that is an essential constituent, necessary component or appropriate ingredient of responsible, relevant, meaningful, effective and beneficial psychotherapy/counseling as traditionally and conventionally practiced. Attributing causality, agency, potency and efficacy to a Superordinate Reality, e.g., Tao, or to a Higher Power, e.g., God; do not involve abdicating professional responsibility and accountability for the nature, characteristics, conduct, proceeding, effects, results, outcomes and consequences of reflections, interpretations, feedback, activities, interactions, actions and interventions in the attending relationship/process. Rather, authentic responsibility and accountability exist to a greater degree, at a higher level and to a fuller extent when true attenders are free of ego-needs, investments and attachments, regardless of the particular nature, focus and forms of the psychotherapeutic work.

Patients/Counselees

In the psychotherapeutic commentaries of this rendition, so-called patients, counselees and clients have simply been referred to as human beings and/or human beings who are engaged in the attending relationship/process of psychotherapy/counseling. For many different reasons, in some way interested, needful and/or vulnerable human beings who are feeling that they are lacking sufficiently adequate personal and/or interpersonal resources to either cope and deal with or to improve and optimize their lives and who believe or hope that they may benefit from professional assistance, often seek out psychotherapists, counselors and therapists who are practicing psychotherapy/counseling.

For such human beings engaging in the attending relationship/process, it is desirable and advisable for them to educate themselves about, and to familiarize themselves with, human nature, psychology, emotions, motivation and behavior; how the mind-body-Spirit unity works; interpersonal relationships, etc., so that they can take as much responsibility for their care as possible and not blindly, unquestioningly, uncritically and necessarily believe and/or accept what authority figures with imputed knowledge, accorded status and apparent power may say, suggest, advise, recommend or prescribe.

Particularly vulnerable human beings are those who are:
- ❖ Afraid of dying, being or becoming mentally ill or physically and socially incapacitated.
- ❖ Intolerant of pain and symptoms of fear, anxiety, depression, grief, anger and other so-called negative physical conditions, mental states, emotional feelings, behavioral actions and/or psychopathological, psychiatric or medical

conditions, diseases, illnesses, disorders and disabilities.
- ❖ Victims and survivors of neglect, trauma and abandonment; incest, rape and violence; physical, emotional and sexual abuse; kidnapping, trafficking and enslavement; terrorism, imprisonment and torture and suffering crippling, disabling and devastating experiences.
- ❖ Suffering from/with psychotic delusions/hallucinations, PTSD flashbacks/nightmares, bipolar energetic cyclings, suicidal ideation/impulses and chronic/terminal physical illnesses.
- ❖ Stigmatized, marginalized, infantalized, patronized, pathologized, criminalized, demonized and otherwise depersonalized, dehumanized, disenfranchised, despirited, invalidated and negated.
- ❖ Socially isolated from family, relatives, friends and other human beings and caregiving resources who might assist them in truly beneficial ways rather than only sympathizing, rationalizing, projecting onto and blaming others and/or meeting their own needs.
- ❖ Experiencing socially conditioned poor self-image, negative self-concept, low self-esteem, diminished self-worth and chronic and debilitating feelings of insecurity, inadequacy, insufficiency, inferiority, incompetency and failure.
- ❖ Habitually and compulsively dependent upon and addicted to various drugs, substances, medications, maladaptive behaviors, conflicted relationships and dysfunctional lifestyles.
- ❖ Unfamiliar with mind-body-Spirit interrelationships, their essential Soul-nature and human Spirit and the healing and transformative power of human Consciousness and psychospiritual energy.
- ❖ Out of touch with or distrusting of basic needs, organismic processes, natural instincts, gut-level sensings, intuitive feelings, inner wisdom, common sense and the simple realities and truths of themselves and their individual lives.

Other than those human beings mandated to, or referred for, psychotherapeutic treatment, the utilizing of the resources and opportunities of an attending relationship/process is made by human beings voluntarily seeking professional assistance for dealing with and resolving their psychological issues, and by those human beings who are interested in personal growth and optimizing the quality of their life through Spiritual and Soul-oriented work.

Psychotherapists/Counselors

In the psychotherapeutic commentaries of this rendition, psychotherapists/counselors are referred to as true attenders. True attenders are truly human beings who have honored, responded to and accepted a vocational calling to serve and to be of encouragement, support, assistance, guidance and benefit to fellow human beings within the context, structure, medium and conduct of the professional practice of the attending relationship/process of psychotherapy/counseling.

It is incumbant upon true attenders to be actively and currently involved in psychotherapeutic and psychospiritual activities that promote self-awareness and understanding; ego-disidentification; Self-actualization and transformation; equality, impartiality and empathy in relation to human beings; awakening to nondual and integral consciousness; truly being an authentic human being and truly living an authentic human life and conducting the attending relationship/process in an appropriate, responsible, ethical, moral, truthful and accountable manner that is free of needs to control, force, manipulate, use or exploit human beings for ego-gratification, self-interest, personal validation, professional status and/or financial gain.

It is essential that true attenders create, secure, sustain and ensure a condition of safety and an atmosphere of trust; structure the attending relationship/process openly, intersubjectively and co-creatively and conduct it consensually, cooperatively and collaboratively with personal transparency, availability and accessibility and human compassion as well as technical expertise. Human beings are to be openly welcomed, received, accepted and acknowledged; listened, attended and related to with dignity, respect, interest, concern and caring and responded to and communicated to with warmth, genuineness, friendliness, goodness, kindness, gentleness and appropriateness.

Attentive being, receptive listening, empathic attuning and responsive entraining are the open psychotherapeutic context and matrix in which a deep connection is made with human beings and from which clear awarenesses occur that naturally flow into the essential, necessary and appropriate conduct of the attending relationship/process in forms, interactions, activities and ways that are experienced by both true attenders and human beings engaged in the attending relationship/process as relevant, meaningful, effective, beneficial and useful.

Preparedness for meeting with human beings in the attending relationship/process entails true attenders clearing their mind, emptying their heart, stilling their will and unifying their being in order to be deeply and fully present, available, accessible and receptive inwardly and outwardly. Ideally, they are free of preconceptions, presuppositions, expectations and anticipations that interfere with their openness to receive and respond to unique human beings just *as* they are presenting themselves. Being so, opens the way, and constitutes an experiential readiness, to be present for and to meet and join with whatever experiences and events are entering and unfolding in the situation, relationship and/or in their field of conscious awareness in the here-now moment.

When true attenders can find the human beings with whom they are meeting within their heart-minds; when they are deeply and fully identified with and are consciously being, living and sharing the blessed gift and precious treasure of human life and when they are Spiritually awakened and Soulfully present, we have a true psychotherapeutic attender and a true psychotherapeutic attending relationship/process.

Practical Applications

The eight principal experiential concepts in this rendition can be applied to the attending relationship/process and can provide a supplementary, complementary, alternative and integrative way of understanding, conducting and experiencing it. The potential usefulness of each one of the eight princpal experiential concepts of Tao, Te, Ch'i, Yin/Yang Ch'i, Wu Wei Ch'i, Tzu Jan, Wan Wu and Chen Jen is presented in summary, synoptic, comparative and tabular forms.

Summaries

Tao/Ultimate Reality

Tao provides a principle and paradigm that includes Spirit, Essence, Being and Self and the Ultimate Reality of the originating Mystery, forming Miracles, manifesting Marvels and completing Magnificence of human being and existence.

Tao provides an encompassing, inclusive, superordinate, transpersonal and integral context, field and framework for the attending relationship/process that are ultimate, absolute and nondual and that integrate the transcendent reality and immanent actualities of human living and the transpersonal dimensions and personal-interpersonal spheres of the human being-together of true attenders and the human beings engaged in it.

Te/Potent Virtuosity

Te provides a model of presence and power that prioritizes the absolutely unique individuality, integrity, inner Tao-nature, authenticity, potency, efficacy, Virtuosity, excellence and genius of human beings rather than exclusively or predominantly regarding them as examples of purely reductive psychological concepts, theories, understandings, profiles and 'cases'.

In addition to the power of the professional standards, ethics, responsibilities, structure, limits, boundaries and procedures of the attending relationship/process; Te provides an understanding of human nature, being, existence and experience solidly grounded and clearly centered in the power of presence rather than the presence of power. It also includes awakening to Spirit and Soul and states of consciousness that transcend usual mental-cognitive operations and intellectual insights and are more intuitive, illuminative and enlightening in nature.

Ch'i/Vital Energy

Ch'i affords the practice of the attending relationship/process with a model of energy and energetic phenomena and operations of human energy that complements formulations of, e.g., psychic energy, orgone energy, bioenergy, energy fields and the workings of energy in affect modulating and self-regulating.

Ch'i is both nonmaterial cosmic energy and material vital energy and constitutes and pervades everything in the universe in varying degrees and at varying levels of condensed vibrational frequencies. Consideration is given to the quantity and quality, circulating and flowing, fluctuating and transforming, balancing and harmonizing and cultivating and conserving of human energy.

Health and vibrancy are freely flowing, fully circulating, naturally compensating and harmoniously balancing Ch'i energy. Fatigue and weakness are decreased, diminished, drained, dissipated and depleted Ch'i energy. Illness and deadness are blocked, obstructed, imbalanced, stuck and frozen Ch'i energy. And death is the complete cessation, absence and lack of Ch'i energy.

Ch'i energy can be cultivated by reserving, conserving and preserving it through:

- ❖ Not leaking, draining, dissipating, wasting, squandering and losing it.
- ❖ Recovering, restoring, replenishing, renewing and reactivating it.

❖ Accumulating, compounding, transforming and properly circulating it.

Nourishing, economizing and modulating Ch'i energy sustain health, immunity and longevity; maintain the ongoing experience of viability, vitality, vibrancy and aliveness; and avoid burning out and the wasting of Ch'i energy in activities, endeavors, behaviors and relationships that are:

❖ Needless, pointless, meaningless, fruitless and worthless.
❖ Extraneous, extreme, excessive, extravagant and indulgent.
❖ Irrelevant, inefficient, ineffective, futile and hopeless.
❖ Overdone, unnecessary, insignificant and unimportant.

Ch'i energy is the bipolarity, alternating, reciprocating and reversing of Yin/Yang dynamics and the flowing, circulating, cycling and returning of Wu Wei kinetics.

Yin/Yang Ch'i/Dynamic Bipolarity

Yin/Yang Ch'i provides a model of polarity and parity that explicitly identifies human existence and experience as bipolar in nature as characterized by an infinite number of mutually interdependent and equally complementary phenomena that are continually interacting, interchanging, transforming, alternating, compensating, counterbalancing, centering, voiding and reversing.

Such a dynamic bipolar model has extensive application to intrapsychic and interpersonal relationships; the change process; critical developmental junctures; the natural rhythms of feeling and activity; transformations occurring within consciousness and awareness; the multitude of bipolar conceptions in the attending relationship/process such as unconcious-conscious, intrapychic-interpersonal, nonverbal-verbal, nondirective-directive, introjection-projection, Self-ego, archetype-complex, introverion-extroversion, body-mind, health-illness and the intersubjective relationship between true attenders and human beings engaged in the attending relationship/process.

Yin/Yang Ch'i alternating dynamics are governed by the Law of Reversal such that when one pole of a bipolar unity reaches its maximum limit, it naturally reverses to its complementary counterpart. Many psychological symptoms, conditions and issues, when fully experienced (which often may be difficult to do) automatically revert to their opposite form, e.g., in a so-called 'healing crisis' or when a fever breaks, a depression lifts, a conflict resolves, a tension releases, an illness runs its course, etc..

Wu Wei Ch'i/Kinetic Fluidity

Wu Wei Ch'i provides a way of considering process and proceeding in the life of the attending relationship/process; its sequential originating, progressing and terminating; its seamless, frictionless and effortless flowing and unfolding and the continuous ongoingness of its many activities, interactions, events and experiences.

The attending relationship/process should be non-intrusive, non-invasive, non-manipulative and non-exploitive. It can be experienced and understood as a Tao-sourced flowing along flexibly, fluidly, naturally, necessarily and appropriately from the clear awareness and experiencing of often unmotivated, unplanned and non-strategic interactions and interventions. Aims, goals, objectives and directions and methods, techniques, processes and procedures are often generated spontaneously and freely and effects, results, outcomes and completions often occur naturally and harmoniously from the fundamentally encouraging, reflecting, supporting, assisting, non-directing, facilitating and guiding approaches of true attenders.

The interactions and interventions made in the attending relationship/process are essential, necessary, responsive and appropriate and are conducted efficiently and effectively through allowing, yielding, following, cooperating, collaborating and accompanying; free of status differentials, defensive resistances, power struggles and acting-out. Wu Wei Ch'i flowing kinetics are governed by the Law of Return such that their proceeding is nonlinear, continuously circulating and cycling and ultimately returning to the origin of its inception of experiences, e.g., when initial presenting issues often re-emerge near/at the time of termination.

Tzu Jan/Natural Spontaneity

Tzu Jan affords a consideration of and appreciation for the spontaneous and serendipitous happenings that naturally occur in the conduct and during the course of the attending relationship/process independent of intentional pre-planning and pre-meditating, contriving and devising, rehearsing and replaying, implementing and executing.

These are the original, creative and innovative; novel, fresh and alive occurrences and experiences that are the presencing and 'playing' of the attending relationship/process; its improvisation, unanticipated surprises, 'ahas' and epiphanies. These *impromptu* and extemporaneous *ad libs* occur concretely, directly and immediately *in situ* and *in vivo* in the here-now moment and are a shared, joyful, delightful and celebratory occasion for both true attenders and the human beings engaged in the attending relationship/process as they are taken by and participating in the vital natural 'playing' of human being, life and experience within their intersubjective consciousness and interhuman relationship.

Wan Wu/Phenomenal Totality

Wan Wu speaks to the richly varied phenomenality and diverse panoramic array of the actuality and totality of the myriad contents, objects, activities and events within the human existence, consciousness, awareness and experience of true attenders and the human beings engaged in the attending relationship/process that are occurring and presenting at any given moment in the time-space of its reality.

Wan Wu are the multiplicity, plurality, variety and diversity of the content, material, data, 'stuff' and '10,000 things' of the attending relationship/process experience that are situated, objectified, identified and experienced as its phenomena. Wan Wu are the concluding, completing, consummating and culminating of the intimate actualities of immanent Tao as things, objects, entities and beings and of thoughts, feelings, behaviors and interactions that are experienced as the richness, fullness and wholeness of the attending relationship/process; being microcosmic holographic presencings, instants and correspondences of/*as* the Ultimate Reality of transcendent Tao.

CHEN JEN/TRULY HUMAN BEING

Chen Jen affords a way of regarding the personhood, partnership and participation of true attenders and the human beings engaged in the professional conduct of the attending relationship/process by considering it to be, first and foremost, a synchronistic dialogical meeting of two human beings and not only a more formal 'doctor-patient' arranged relationship.

The characteristics, attributes and qualities of Chen Jen are embodiments of what it is and means to be a true, genuine, authentic and real human being and to personify being Tao-like in its Virtuosity/Te, dynamic-kinetic operations of Yin/Yang and Wu Wei Ch'i and the spontaneous presencing/Tzu Jan of its experiential phenomena/Wan Wu.

As Chen Jen, ideally, true attenders are disidentified from ego-images, self-concepts and professional personas and are Tao-focused and centered, Tao-embodied and personified, and Tao-identified; purely and simply, sheerly and utterly alive, unique human beings who are experiencing and sharing the precious blessing, gift, treasure and opportunity of human life, being and existence. They are present, open and transparent, available and accessible, committed and connected, engaged and involved and participating and communing.

Synopses

The following are synopses of the eight principal experiential concepts and some of the salient characteristics and complementary activities of true attenders and the attending relationship/process toward which they point.

TE/POTENT VIRTUOSITY

- Cognitive/thinking/knowing mode/non-thinking/non-knowing/Tao-knowing.
- Letting-be/respecting/witnessing/beholding/acknowledging/appreciating.
- Receiving/exploring/discovering/illuminating/enlightening/awakening.
- Non presupposing/preconceiving/assuming/predetermining.
- Non reducing experiences to an exclusively psychological understanding.
- Not only abstracting/construing/defining/labeling/classifying/categorizing.
- Not only analyzing/interpreting/determining/concluding/explaining.
- Not only concepts/theories/data/symptom pictures/clinical descriptions.
- Not only psychogenesis/psychodynamics/psychopathology/psychodiagnosis.

YIN/YANGCH'I/DYNAMIC BIPOLARITY

- Affective/feeling/having mode/non-desiring/non-having/Tao-having
- Letting-go/relinquishing/not pursuing/acquiring/possessing/displaying.
- Reflecting/attuning/according/interchanging/alternating/reversing.

- ❖ Non investing in/attaching to preferred/favorite theories/techniques.
- ❖ Non comparing/conflating/confusing similar clinical issues and 'cases'.
- ❖ Not only clinical assessing/evaluating/judgments/case formulating.
- ❖ Not only mutually exclusive/either-or/one-sided/dualistic opposites.
- ❖ Not only employing standard/familiar/routine repertoires of interactions.
- ❖ Not only encouraging affective/emotional expression/release/catharsis.

Wu Wei Ch'i/Kinetic Fluidity

- ❖ Conative/acting/doing mode/non-acting/non-doing/Tao-doing.
- ❖ Going-with/re-sourcing/sourcing activity in Tao/Consciousness.
- ❖ Responding/yielding/complying/allowing/following/accompanying.
- ❖ Non interfering with the ongoing naturally unfolding process.
- ❖ Non controlling/managing/manipulating/directing/forcing actions.
- ❖ Not only treatment planning/goal-setting/intervention strategizing.
- ❖ Not only working with defenses/resistances/power struggles/acting-out.
- ❖ Not only implementing treatment techniques for specific outcomes.
- ❖ Not only a treatment model of tactics/operations/maneuvers/campaigns.

Tao/Ultimate Reality

- Unitive/relating/being mode/non-existing/non-being/Tao-being.
- Being-with/residing/joining/connecting/uniting/integrating/communing.
- Returning/synchronistic meeting/affiliating/therapeutic alliance/interbeing.
- Non separating/dividing/isolating/distancing/alienating/fragmenting.
- Non objectifying/stereotyping/stigmatizing/marginalizing/infantalizing.
- Not only professional persona/status differential/authoritative demeanor.
- Not only working with transference/countertransference projections.
- Not only outcome evaluating/termination determining/closing focus.
- Not only reviewing the attending relationship/any unfinished business.

Ch'i/Vital Energy

- Activating/nourishing/sustaining/life-force/viability/vitality/vibrancy.
- Allowing energy to naturally compensate/self-correct/balance/circulate.
- Not necessarily attempting to manipulate/change energy by freeing stuck/blocked energy, collecting drained/dissipated energy, focusing scattered/deviated energy, redirecting diverted/deflected energy, integrating divided/fragmented energy, stimulating low/weak energy, activating congealed/sluggish energy, modulating high/intense energy or balancing antagonistic/conflicted energy.

Tzu Jan/Natural Spontaneity

- ❖ Naturalness/spontaneity/serendipity/happening/surprise/automatic presencing.
- ❖ Phenomenal presencing/manifesting/appearing of-itself-so/just-*as*-it-is/self-so.
- ❖ Improvised/*ad lib*/extemporaneous/creative/innovative/alive/fresh expressions.
- ❖ Non preplanning/pre-meditating/pre-arranging actions/activities/programs.
- ❖ Non replicating/repeating/replaying/redoing/re-enacting/reprising procedures.
- ❖ Non reviewing/rehearsing/practicing/staging/performing 'canned' routines.

Wan Wu/Phenomenal Totality

- ❖ Blessings/gifts/treasures/Mysteries/Miracles/Marvels/Magnificence of Tao.
- ❖ Phenomena as immanent/holographic correspondences of transcendent Tao.
- ❖ Non abstracting/externalizing/objectifying contents/goods/deeds/others/things.
- ❖ Non separated and divided fragments/pieces/parts/bits/bytes/facts/data.
- ❖ Not only dilemmas/questions/conflicts/problems/issues/concerns/'material'.
- ❖ Not only ideas/thoughts/emotions/feelings/actions/behaviors/relationships.
- ❖ Not only conditions/situations/circumstances/matters/affairs/events/'business'.
- ❖ Not only concepts/theories/techniques/methods/interactions/interventions.

Chen Jen/Truly Human Being

- True/genuine/authentic/real/honest/upright/straightforward/trustworthy human being.
- Open/available/accessible/interested/connected/engaged/involved/participating.
- Attending/co-creating/collaborating/intersubjective and interhuman dialoguing.
- Non rigid/inflexible rules/ranks/roles/rituals/recipes/regimens/rigamaroles.
- Non formulas/prescriptions/lectures/monologues/intellectualized discussions.
- Not only professional persona and demeanor/confidently authoritative figure.
- Not only proficient theoretician/competent technician/skillful practitioner.
- Embodying/personifying/enacting/identifying *as* the qualities of the Ultimate Reality and intimate actualities of Tao; the unique individuality, Virtuosity and efficacious power of Te; the bipolar, alternating, reciprocating and reversing dynamics of Yin/Yang Ch'i; the flowing, circulating, cycling and returning kinetics of Wu Wei Ch'i; the natural, spontaneous, free and full presencing of Tzu Jan and the myriad, varied, diverse and complete phenomena of Wan Wu.

Comparisons

The following material identifies and compares some of the 'more' and 'less' characteristics of the eight principal experiential concepts as they might relate and apply to true attenders and human beings engaged in the attending relationship/process.

Te/Potent Virtuosity

Less knowing *'about'*
Presupposing/preconceiving/presuming
Abstracting/construing/defining
Analyzing/interpreting/formulating
Classifying/categorizing/labeling
Conceptualizing/theorizing/concluding
Speculating/hypothesizing/prognosticating
Diagnosing/pathologizing/determining
Verbalizing/explaining/lecturing

More letting-be/knowing no-'thing'/mental 'contents'
Beholding/witnessing/observing
Welcoming/receiving/accepting
Regarding/acknowledging/appreciating
Attending/listening/wondering
Gathering/inquiring/clarifying
Considering/describing/feeding back
Exploring/discovering/experiencing
Discerning/comprehending/understanding

Yin/Yang Ch'i/Dynamic Bipolarity

Less having *'of'*
Assessing/appraising/evaluating
Ranking/weighting/rating
Status differential/top-down hierarchy
Clinical judgment/selectivity/valuation
Associating of familiar 'cases'/issues
Attaching to preferred theories/methods
One-sided/mutually exclusive dualities
Seeking/pursuing/acquiring
Claiming/retaining/displaying

More letting-go/having no-'thing'/emotional 'goods'
Adjusting/adapting/accomodating
Aligning with/attuning to/according with
Complementary/interdependent bipolarities
Mutuality/equality/impartiality
Alternating/reciprocating/reversing
Focusing on changing/transforming
Reflecting/paraphrasing/empathizing
Interacting/interchanging/exchanging
Balancing/equalizing/harmonizing
Self-regulating/centering/stabilizing
Divesting/detaching/relinquishing

WU WEI CH'I/KINETIC FLUIDITY

Less doing *'to'*
Imposing/interfering/intervening
Initiating/asserting/confronting
Planning/agendas/programs
Devising/implementing/executing
Contriving/strategizing/treating
Aims/goals/objectives/purposes
Effects/results/outcomes
Prescriptive/formulaic/standardized
Methods/techniques/procedures
Controlling/leading/directing
Structuring/managing/manipulating
Challenging/forcing/coercing
Reacting/conflicting/contending
Striving/efforting/struggling
Defending/resisting/acting-out

More going-with/doing no-'thing'/volitional 'deeds'
Trusting/allowing/following
Conforming/complying/cooperating

Encouraging/supporting/coaching
Assisting/facilitating/guiding
Grounding/stabilizing/calming
Flexing/yielding/flowing
Seamless/frictionless/effortless
Adventuring/journeying/wandering
Suggesting/experimenting/trying-out
Developing/unfolding/proceeding
Responding/reinforcing/accompanying
Sourcing/cycling/returning
Collaborating/synergy/co-creating
Appropriate actions following awareness

Tao/Ultimate Reality

Less being-'*apart*'
Conventional/orthodox/official
Authority/persona/image
Screening/selecting/excluding
Separating/dividing/isolating
Distancing/alienating/dissociating
Externalizing/objectifying/reducing
Limiting/restricting/constraining
Fragmenting/partializing/fractionating
Stereotyping/projecting/transferring
Unilateral monologuing/relating
End-setting/outcome evaluating
Reviewing progress/determining termination

More being-with/being no-'thing'/relational 'others'
Meeting/engaging/involving
Co-existing/joining/connecting
Affiliating/associating/allying
Including/abiding/communing
Mutuality/sharing/participating

Realness/naturalness/freeness
Openness/disclosing/transparency
Congruence/intersubjectivity/dialoguing
Synthesizing/integrating/unifying
Fullness/wholeness/completeness
Journeying/wayfaring/sojourning
Spiritual/transpersonal context

CH'I/VITAL ENERGY

Less devitalizing
Blocked/obstructed/stuck
Leaked/drained/dissipated
Consumed/wasted/squandered
Weakened/depleted/exhausted
Diverted/displaced/scattered
Hindered/hampered/impeded
Dampened/suppressed/repressed
Uncontrolled/unregulated/unmodulated
Congealed/coagulated/sluggish
Amplified/intense/overwhelming

More vitalizing
Reserved/conserved/preserved
Available/accessible/utilizable
Cultivated/nourished/compounded
Focused/channeled/directed
Shifting/compensating/self-correcting
Balancing/centering/stabilizing
Changing/transforming/transmuting
Flowing/circulating/cycling
Recovering/restoring/replenishing
Revitalizing/renewing/rejuvenating

Tzu Jan/Natural Spontaneity

Less unnatural
Pre-planned/pre-meditated/pre-figured
Artificial/fabricated/manufactured
Reproduced/replicated/re-created
Repeated/replayed/re-enacted
Rehearsed/practiced/prepared
Produced/directed/performed
Routine/habitual/customary
Derived/conditioned/dependent
Abstract/indirect/mediated
Trite/stale/hackneyed

More just-so/*as*-is
Natural/spontaneous/free
Original/creative/innovative
Improvised/*impromptu*/*ad lib*
Unintended/serendipitous/surprising
Presencing/happening/random
Concrete/direct/immediate
Sui generis/*ipso facto*/*in vivo*/*in situ*
Of-itself-so/self-so/self-like
New/fresh/alive

Wan Wu/Phenomenal Totality

Less 'things'
Contents/goods/deeds
Egos/others/whos
Its/thats/those
Hers/hims/them
Facts/data/'material'
Parts/pieces/bits
Events/affairs/matters
Effects/results/outcomes

Products/possessions/property
Situations/occasions/occurrences
Masses/herds/ciphers

More phenomena
Beings/existents/entities
Human beings/Selves/Souls
Dimensions/realms/states
This/these/here-now
Multiplicity/plurality/diversity
Wholes/unities/integers
Myriad/innumerable/countless
Bestowals/blessings/gifts
Riches/bounty/treasures
Wonders/Miracles/Marvels
Ordinary/everyday experiences

CHEN JEN/TRULY HUMAN BEING

Less ego-like
Ego-/self-/personality-identified
Role-/function-/status-identified
Doctor-/psychotherapist-patient
Counselor-/therapist-client
Authority figure/persona/image
Official/formal/impersonal
Orthodox/traditional/conventional
Yang-like/Wei-like

More Being-like
True/genuine/authentic/real
Natural/universal/ordinary
Fellow wayfaring companion
Tao-focused/Tao-centered
Tao-embodying/Tao-personifying
Tao-realizing/Tao-actualizing

Tao-returning/Tao-identifying
Te-/Yin Yang Ch'i-/Wu Wei Ch'i-like
Tzu Jan-/Wan Wu-/Chen Jen-like
Yin-like/Wu-/Yu-state-like
Spirit-/Self-/Soul-like

Table Two

The following table includes the four principal experiential concepts of Te, Yin/Yang Ch'i, Wu Wei Ch'i and Tao and their respective applications to some traditional focuses, activities and self-qualities and to some complementary focuses, activities and end-states that relate to the structure, characteristics, conduct and fruition of the attending relationship/process.

Concept   TE/POTENT VIRTUOSITY
Modality   *Thinking/conceiving/knowing*
           Cognitive/mental
           Structure/content/potency

Some traditional focuses and activities:
    Presenting issues/symptoms
    Intake interviewing
    Behavioral observation
    History taking/data gathering
    Psychogenic etiology
    Ego-strengths/coping skills
    Self-concept/personal power
    Diagnostic assessment
    Nosological classifying
    Prognostic assessment

Attending/listening/observing
Abstracting/analyzing/interpreting
Defining/labeling/categorizing
Insight/explaining

Self-characteristics:
Self-respecting/awareness
Self-acceptance/appreciation
Self-knowledge/understanding
Self-individuating/empowering
Self-realizing/awakening
Self-concept/idea

Some complementary focuses and activities:
Not rigid recipes/rubrics/rules
Welcoming/acknowledging/accepting
Witnessing/beholding/appreciating
Respecting/receiving/not rejecting
Letting-be/abstaining

Attention to:
Mystery of originating/creating
Conception
Authenticity/integrity
Inner truth
Potency/efficacy
Virtuosity/genius

Sincerity/sagacity
Uniqueness/inwardness/trueness

End-States:
Tao-awakened/realized/embodied
Truth/wisdom/Light

Concept	**Yin/Yang Ch'i/Dynamic Bipolarity**
Modality	*Feeling/desiring/having*
	Affective/emotional
	Organization/form/polarity

Some traditional focuses and activities:
  Case formulating
  Needs/resources assessment
  Ego-defenses/resistances
  Affect-regulating
  Adaptiveness/resiliency
  Intrapsychic/interpersonal dynamics
  Choices/conflicts/changes
  Rapport building
  Status hierarchies
  Clinical judgments

  Evaluating/assessing/appraising
  Investing/preferring/attaching
  Comparing/associating/judging
  Catharsis/expressing

Self-characteristics:
  Self-reflecting/evaluating
  Self-organizing/regulating
  Self-compensating/correcting
  Self-balancing/centering
  Self-owning/transforming
  Self-esteem/worth

Some complementary focuses and activities:
  Not rigid ranks/ratings/repertoires
  Aligning/attuning/according
  Adjusting/adapting/accomodating
  Reflecting/releasing/not retaining
  Letting-go/relinquishing

Attendant with:
    Miracles of forming/transforming
    Gestation
    Equality/impartiality
    Interdependence/complementarity
    Mutuality/reciprocity
    Emergency/transiency

    Simplicity/sufficiency
    Harmony/beauty/goodness

End States:
    Tao-centered/assimilated/attained
    Good/harmony/Love

Concept	Wu Wei Ch'i/Kinetic Fluidity
Modality	*Doing/acting/making*
	Conative/volitional
	Function/operation/process

Some traditional focuses and activities:
    Treatment planning
    Goal-setting
    Intervention strategizing
    Methodological techniques
    Therapeutic cooperation
    Impulse control
    Working with defenses/resistances
    Working through power struggles
    Behavioral 'experimenting'
    Determining effectiveness

    Supporting/assisting/facilitating
    Interacting/intervening
    Defenses/resistances/struggles
    Working through/redoing

Self-characteristics:
    Self-creating/generating
    Self-controlling/asserting
    Self-supporting/directing
    Self-determining/actualizing
    Self-developing/self-relying
    Self-confidence/mastery

Some complementary focuses and activities:
    Not rigid rites/rituals/regimens
    Agreeing/acceding/allowing
    Yielding/following/accompanying
    Responding/replying/not reacting
    Going-with/sourcing

Attending to:
    Marvels of manifesting/actualizing
    Parturition
    Flexibility/fluidity
    Frictionlessness/effortlessness
    Originality/creativity
    Collaborating/co-creating

    Synergy/serenity
    Appropriateness/gracefulness/rightness

End-states:
    Tao-sourced/enacted/actualized
    Right/peace/Law

Concept   Tao/Ultimate Reality
Modality *Being/existing/living*
              Unitive/relational
              Relation/context/principle

Some traditional focuses and activities:
    Interpersonal relationships
    Transference/countertransference
    Intimacy issues
    Prognostic considerations
    End-setting
    Outcome evaluating
    Termination determining
    Unfinished business
    Treatment closure
    Future meetings

    Availability/self-disclosing
    Intersubjective relating
    Communicating/dialoguing
    Therapeutic alliance

Self-characteristics:
    Self-existing/revealing
    Self-integrating/identifying
    Self-completing/fulfilling
    Self-liberating/transcending
    Self-giving/contributing
    Self-identity/ideal

Some complementary focuses and activities:
    Not rigid rights/roles/regalia
    Associating/affiliating/allying
    Connecting/abiding/communing
    Reuniting/residing/not restricting
    Being-with/joining

Attender at:
   Magnificence of completing/fulfilling
   Maturation
   Unity/community
   Universality/totality
   Consummating/culminating
   Intimacy/liberty

   Spontaneity/Spirituality
   Oneness/wholeness/completeness

End-States:
   Tao-returned/identified/completed
   Reality/freedom/Life

Psychopathology

It may be of interest and heuristic value to identify some of the symptoms, states, conditions, behaviors, etc. typically worked with in the attending relationship/process and relate them to the four principal experiential concepts of Te, Yin/Yang Ch'i, Wu Wei Ch'i and Tao.

Concept	TE/POTENT VIRTUOSITY	YIN/YANG CH'I/DYNAMIC BIPOLARITY
Modality	Mental/cognitive Thinking/knowing	Emotional/affective Feeling/having
Issue	Ignoring	Attaching
Medium	Beliefs/hopes Fantasies/dreams	Needs/wishes Desires/wants

	Rationality/potency	Equality/harmony
Lack of		
Symptoms	Insanity	Emptiness
States	Craziness	Worthlessness
Conditions	Madness	Poverty
Behaviors	Hallucinations	Despair
	Flashbacks	Bipolar Cycling
	Delusions	Anhedonia
	Irrationality	Dependency
	Misinterpretation	Addiction
	Fears	Anxieties
	Pain	Depression
	Guilt	Grief
	Shame	Loss
	Worries	Conflicts
	Confusion	Anger
	Doubts	Frustration
	Regrets	Stress
	Projections	Tensions
	Obsessions	Discontent
	Dishonesty	Devaluation
	Inauthenticity	Inequality
	Phoniness	Deficiency
	Badness	Insufficiency
	Stupidity	Inferiority
	Insignificance	Immaturity
	Invalidity	Inadequacy
	Powerlessness	Insecurity

Concept	Wu Wei Ch'i/ Kinetic Fluidity	Tao/ Ultimate Reality
Modality	Volitional/conative Acting/doing	Relational/unitive Co-existing/being
Issue	Erring	Separating
Medium	Habits/drives Tendencies/impulses	Splits/divides Fragments/binds
Lack of	Agency/mastery	Unity/intimacy
Symptoms	Failure	Isolation
States	Mistakes	Alienation
Conditions	Weakness	Dissociation
Behaviors	Impotence Incompetence Ineptness Ineffectiveness Suicidality Panic Defeat Domination Manipulation Exploitation Struggle Agitation Abuse Violence Compulsions	Loneliness Fragmentation Incompleteness Unreality Disorientation Distance Exclusion Dismissal Neglect Abandonment Restriction Constraint Invalidation Prejudice Negation

Stuckness   Infantalization
Rigidity   Patronization
Passivity   Stigmatization
Indolence   Marginalization
Wrongness   Pathologization
Helplessness   Criminalization
Impulsivity   Victimization
Rebelliousness   Dehumanization

T'IEN
天

Heaven/celestial
Sky/material heavens
Highest/vast space
Anthropomorphic diety
Supreme Ruler/God
Day/weather/season
Nature (with Earth)

TI
地

Earth/terrestrial
Soil/land
Ground/floor
Fields/territory
Place/location
Position/situation
Nature/(with Heaven)

LIEN

Connect/join/link
Associate/ally
Combine/unite

LIEN

Connect/join/link
Together with/also
Include/continue

Heaven-Earth is synonymous with Nature and is the connecting, joining and integrating of the celestial and terrestrial dimensions of Reality, of the sky and the soil. Human Being is the connecting link that joins Heaven and Earth, spiritually and materially. The True Human Being/Chen Jen mediates Heaven-Earth, is a companion of the two, respectively embodies both as the Spiritual/Hun Soul and the physical/P'o Soul in the head and belly energy centers and integrates both in the Heart energy center of the human body.

APPENDIX ONE

The following are paraphrased abridgements of, and psychotherapeutic commentaries on, additional tales from Outer Records 19, 20 and 22 and Miscellaneous Records 24, 26, 28 and 32 of *The Chuang Tzu* text that further illustrate the nature, characteristics, qualities and activities of True human beings that can be generalized and applied to those of true attenders in the attending relationship/process.

TALES FROM THE OUTER/MISCELLANEOUS RECORDS

RECORD 19
Mastering Life

❖ THE CICADA CATCHER

TEXT

A Master-Sage is happening upon a hunchbacked woman who is easily catching cicadas on the tip of a sticky pole and exclaims, 'What skill! Is there a special way to it?' The cicada catcher replies, 'Yes, I have a way. First, I balance two balls on top of each other on the end of this pole, then three and then five. If five balls do not fall off, then I know that I will not miss any cicadas.

I hold my body upright and still as a tree and use my arm like a straight branch. Many things exist in Heaven, on Earth and in the world but I am only aware of cicadas. Not wavering, I do not let anything else distract me. That is how I catch them.' The Master-Sage reflects, 'You keep your consciousness undivided and concentrate your Spirit. That seems to be how you catch and never miss a cicada.'

Commentary

True attenders are successfully conducting and completing the attending relationship/process by maintaining an upright and still body, steady and straightforward stance and concentrated and undistracted one-pointed consciousness on the work at hand.

❖ The Ferryman

Text

A wayfarer is asking a ferryman, who is appearing to handle his boat with supernatural ability, whether people can learn how to do it. The ferryman answers, 'Certainly! Good swimmers, especially underwater swimmers, can quickly and easily get the hang of it; even if they never have seen a boat before, because they forget the water. To them, water is like dry land and a boat is like a cart. Inwardly, they are unaffected and at ease with whatever they do and wherever they go.'

Commentary

True attenders are effectively navigating the waters of the attending relationship/process and are effortlessly assisting in ferrying human beings from here to there by forgetting its context and medium and by experiencing it as nothing different from their ordinary lives and are inwardly unaffected and at ease.

❖ The Archer

Text

A wayfarer is asking a winning archer about the skill involved. The archer explains, 'In an archery contest, when I am not competing for anything, I naturally shoot accurately. But if I try to win prizes, I worry about my aim. And if I am competing for gold, I get anxious and may not do as well. Because the stakes are greater, I might let external considerations disturb my mind. When overly concerned with the outside, I could get clumsy on the inside.'

Commentary

True attenders are not regarding the attending relationship/process as a competetive contest to win, are not letting external circumstances create worry or anxiety about performing well and are conducting it in a naturally relaxed and graceful manner that does not inwardly affect their aim or accuracy of being on target.

❖ The Rooster Trainer

Text

A rooster trainer is training some roosters to fight. After ten days, the promoter asks if they are ready to fight. The trainer replies, ' Not yet. They are too cocky and rely upon their nerve.' After another ten days the promoter inquires again and the trainer reports, 'Not yet. They are still distracted by noises and movements.' After yet another ten days, the promoter checks again and the trainer reports, 'Not yet. They are still too spirited and looking all around.'

After another ten days, the promoter checks in again and this time the trainer indicates that the roosters are ready to fight. 'When another rooster is crowing, they are not showing any sign of change. Seen from a distance, they appear to be made of wood. Their Virtuosity is complete. Other roosters will not dare to face them and will turn around and run away rather than fight with them.'

Commentary

True attenders are not overconfident, are not distracted by the activities of human beings and changes in the attending relationship/process, are able to focus their energy and to calmly concentrate on the matters at hand without being affected. Their stillness and the efficacious power of their Virtuosity/Te do not create conflicts or power struggles for human beings.

❖ THE SWIMMER

TEXT

A Master-Sage is coming upon a waterfall where the water drops thirty feet and then rushes along for thousands of feet so swiftly that fishes are not able to swim in it. The Master-Sage sees a woman dive into the waters and quickly tries to have her rescued. But she emerges from the waters on her own and proceeds to stroll along the riverside singing a song.

The Master-Sage catches up with her and asks if she has some special way of staying afloat in such rapid currents. The swimmer replies, 'I have no special way. I begin with what I am used to, am one with my own nature and let things come to completion by destiny.

I go under the swirls and come out with the eddies, following along the way the water is going and do not think about myself. That is how I stay afloat.' The Master-Sage asks for clarification and the swimmer explains, 'I was born on dry land and and am used to it. I grew up with water and feel one with and safe in it. And I do not know why or how I am doing what I do. That is destiny!'

COMMENTARY

True attenders are bringing their personal histories, unique identities and extent of self-development to the medium of the attending relationship/process and are joining and safely following along with its process in the ways that it is moving along and completing itself without being self-conscious or necessarily needing to know why it is naturally proceeding and developing in the way that it is.

❖ The Bell Stand Carver

Text

A woodworker is finishing carving wood into a bell stand. The people seeing it are marveling at the quality of the workmanship which seems to be divinely created. When asked about what art he possesses, the bell stand carver replies, 'I am only a craftsperson. I have no art. However, there are a few things. When I am making a bell stand, I never let it wear out my energy. I always fast and quiet my mind. After three days, I do not have any thoughts about recognition or rewards. After five days, I do not have any thoughts about skillfulness or clumsiness, praise or blame. And after seven days; I am so clear, empty and still that I forget my body and limbs.

Then I forget who commissioned the work. I am so concentrated that all considerations and distractions are gone. Then, I go into the forest and contemplate the Heavenly nature of trees. When I see a bell stand in one of them, I start carving it. This way, I am simply matching up Heaven with Heaven, my inborn nature with that of the tree. That is probably why people wonder if the results are divinely created.'

Commentary

True attenders are not letting the art of the attending relationship/process drain their energy by quieting their minds, forgetting about technical skills, detaching from concerns about successful outcomes and professional recognition and are forgetting about themselves and distractions such as referral sources and reasons for referrals. Then, from their clearness, emptiness and stillness; true attenders are contemplating the Heavenly nature and unique inner essence, nature and potentials of human beings engaged in the attending relationship/process. They are attuning to and matching the Heavenly nature of human beings with their own and then are engaging in the divinely creative work of assisting them in carving away all that is not their true nature and realizing who they really and truly are.

❖ Forgetting

Text

An artist is drawing freehand as true as if she is using a ruler or compass because she is letting her hand naturally change with things and is not letting her mind get in the way. Her Spirit is unified and unobstructed. When our shoes fit, we forget our feet. When our belts fit, we forget our waists. When are minds are comfortable, we forget good or bad and right or wrong and have true understanding. There is no change in what is inside and no following of what is outside when adjusting to things is fitting and comfortable. We begin with what is comfortable and do not experience what is uncomfortable when we know the true comfort of forgetting what is comfortable.

Commentary

True attenders are suspending mental, conceptual and theoretical concerns; are Spiritually unified and clear and are allowing themselves to change along with and to harmonize with the attending relationship/process as it naturally unfolds, proceeds and develops. They are aligning with, attuning to and according with human beings; are not experiencing discomfort in appropriate and fitting interactions; are forgetting about good or bad and right or wrong interventions and are in a nondual state of consciousness beyond inner constancy and outer fluctuations and comfort or discomfort.

❖ Nourishing a Bird

Text

A Master is discoursing about some disciples who are confused by descriptions of the Virtuosity of True human beings. 'It is like a wild bird that flies into a ruler's court and the ruler is so delighted that he has an elaborate feast prepared for it complete with music and dance. But the bird is upset and petrified. This is trying to nourish a bird with what might be fitting for a human being. If you want to nourish a bird, let it roost in a deep forest, float on a clear river or feast on tasty snakes. This way it would naturally be at ease. These disciples are as out of place as the bird. Describing the Virtuosity of True human beings to those who are so limited in their understanding is like taking a mouse for a carriage ride or trying to delight a quail with bells and drums. No wonder they are confused.'

Commentary

True attenders are not ignoring or compromising the innate nature of human beings, misjudging their degree of development, projecting their own values onto them or making irrelevant and inappropriate interpretations, interactions or interventions. They are working within the unique individualities and phenomenological frames of reference of human beings and are assisting them in living more adequately, congruently and comfortably in their natural environments and circumstances as quickly as possible.

RECORD 20
The Mountain Tree

❖ The Empty Boat

Text

If people are crossing a river in a boat and an empty boat happens to bump into them, no matter how bad-tempered they may be, they do not usually become angry and simply push the boat out of their way. But if there are other people in the boat, they shout curses and directions at them. In the first instance, they are facing emptiness and in the second instance, they are facing occupancy. When we are empty and wandering in the world, who can harm us?

Commentary

True attenders are egoless, empty and unoccupied with and free of theoretical concepts, diagnostic assessments, case formulations, treatment plans, intervention strategies and outcome expectations as they are wandering in the world, and traversing the waters, of the attending relationship/process. They are thus avoiding running into and bumping up against intense confrontations, conflicted interactions, power struggles, angry transference reactions and physical acting-out.

❖ The Bell Maker

Text

A bell maker is building a bell stand outside of the court gates and the ruler observing the work inquires, 'What art is it that you are commanding?' The bell maker replies, 'In the midst of Oneness, how can I be commanding anything? When the work is completed, I return to simplicity and plainness. Dull, I am without understanding. Calm, I am without purpose. With a sense of mystery and wonder, I let be whatever is coming and let go of whatever is going. What is coming cannot be avoided and what is going cannot be stopped. I follow the aggressive as well as the deferent and let each be as they are and do what they do. This way I encounter no trouble. How much more so is this true of people who have hold of Tao?'

Commentary

True attenders are achieving admirable psychotherapeutic results but are not considering their work to be due to any particular clinical skills, proficiencies and competencies. They are conducting the attending relationship/process in a state of unity, simplicity, calmness and openness and with a sense of mystery, non-knowing, wondering, non-doing and wandering and are accepting the varied positive and negative phenomena occurring within it as they are coming, completing themselves and going.

RECORD 22
Knowledge Wandered North

❖ THE BUCKLE MAKER

TEXT

A buckle maker who is eighty years old has not lost any of her dexterity. Being asked about what skill or special way she has in making buckles, she answers, 'I have a way. Ever since I was twenty years old, I have loved making buckles. I never look at any other things. If it is not a buckle, I do not bother with it. Using this way of not using other things, I am able to get the most use out of it. How much greater would people be if, in the same way, they reached the point where there is nothing that they did not use?'

COMMENTARY

True attenders are typically responding to an early life calling to be engaged in a vocation like that of psychotherapeutic attending, are single-minded in their commitment to it, love working with human beings, tend to exclude whatever is irrelevant to their Heart-of-Hearts vocation and are able to use all of themselves in it.

RECORD 24
The Recluse and the Ruler

❖ Dog and Horse Judging

Text

A recluse is explaining how he judges dogs to a troubled ruler whom he perceives as needing to be cheered up. 'A dog of lowest quality has the nature of a wild dog and is only concerned with catching prey. A dog of average quality appears proud and overconfident. But a dog of highest quality acts as if it has completely lost its identity.

I judge horses in the same way. Horses that are able to gallop straight as a plumb line, arc as smoothly as a French curve, turn as precisely as a T-square and circle as true as a compass; I judge to be worthy enough for a kingdom, but not for the ordinary world. No, no. A horse for the ordinary world is one whose talents are complete. It seems to be absent and unaware of its identity but, in this way, it outruns all of the other horses almost out of sight.' The ruler, unable to take himself and his rulership so seriously, burst out laughing and was cheered up by the simple story of this True human being.

Commentary

True attenders are assisting human beings in their developing from being ego-identified and self-occupied individuals who may feel perfectly accomplished and are overly confident and falsely proud to ones more free of a sense of personal ego-identity and elevated status and freer to develop the natural gifts, talents and genius of their Virtuosity/Te; who do not humorlessly take themselves too seriously and who do not regard their lives so much as a problem to be solved but rather as a life course to be run optimally.

RECORD 26
External Things

❖ Forgotten Words

Text

A fish net and a rabbit trap exist because of fishes and rabbits. Once you have caught the fish or the rabbit, you can forget the net and the trap. Words exist because of meaning. Once you have caught the meaning, you can forget the words. Where can I find a human being who has forgotten words so we can have a word with each other?[19]

Commentary

True attenders are not engaging in excessive verbalizations, are not intentionally and/or strategically employing words as means to ends and are using words to become aware of the meaning of human experience and then forgetting them. They are becoming free of words so that true words are spoken naturally, spontaneously and effortlessly in authentic Heart-to-Heart dialogues with human beings engaged in the attending relationship/process.

RECORD 28
Giving Away a Throne

❖ Double Injury

Text

A ruler is lamenting to a hermit about his own difficulties with trying to live like a hermit. 'My body is here beside the river but my mind is still back at the palace. What can I do about this?' The hermit answers, 'Attach more importance to life. If you regard living itself as important you will forget about material things.' The ruler allows, 'I know that is what I need to do but I cannot overcome my inclinations.' The hermit counters, 'If you cannot overcome your inclinations, then follow them.' The ruler queries, 'But will not that be harming Spirit?' The hermit adds, 'If you cannot overcome your inclinations and then force yourself not to follow them, this does double injury to yourself and will shorten your life.' It is more difficult for a wealthy ruler to retire to a life among the cliffs and caves than it is for an ordinary person to do. Although the ruler did not realize Tao, at least he had the will to do so.

Commentary

True attenders are modeling for human beings a deep commitment to truly valuing the sheer and utter reality of living that overrides, eclipses and displaces relatively less significant ego-states of mind, inclinations, propensities and tendencies and habitual ways of being. If unable to overcome preferences, investments and attachments; they are accepting them and letting them be and run their course rather than forcefully trying to change, suppress or stop them and doubling the injury to their Spirit by adding manipulation to their deviation. Also, they are not necessarily resisting the resistances or disarming the defenses of human beings engaged in the attending relationship/process.

The above additional tales illustrate how true attenders are able to be, to embody, to live and to enact Wu-states of Non-Being, non-knowing, non-having and non-doing and Yu-states of oneness, clearness, emptiness and stillness in their personal lives and in the professional practice of the attending relationship/process.

RECORD 32
Lieh Tzu

❖ CHUANG TZU'S FUNERAL

TEXT

Chuang Tzu is dying and his devoted followers are wanting to give him a grand funeral. But Chuang Tzu responds, 'Heaven-Earth is my coffin, sun and moon are my jade discs, stars and constellations are my pearl beads and the myriad human beings are my farewell gifts. Everything for my funeral is already right here, right now. What else need be added?'

The followers lament, 'But we fear that your body will be eaten by hawks and crows.' Chuang Tzu replies with great humility and impartiality, 'If above ground, I will be eaten by hawks and crows. If below ground, I will be eaten by crickets and ants. How prejudiced of me to deprive one group to supply the other.'

When you use what is biased to achieve fairness, the fairness is unfair. When you use what is false to establish truthfulness, the truthfulness is untrue. Wide-eyed people are no more than servants of things but Spiritual human beings are discovering real truths. Wide-eyed people are no match for human beings of Spirit. That is how it has been since very long ago. Yet foolish people are still believing what they see, are lost in external things and are only accomplishing what is irrelevant. Is not it so sad?

COMMENTARY

True attenders are impartial and equitable to the end in being and working with human beings in a true attending relationship/process. The structure, functions, relationships, activities, conduct and proceedings of a true attending relationship/process are natural to them, already at hand and complete as they are without adding or using irrelevant theories and manipulative techniques to achieve the semblance of true understanding and real results that are any other than those of the natural unfolding, developing, progressing and completing of ordinary authentic human relationships.

True attenders are unbiased and truthful and have a microscopic and telescopic vision that see deeper into and farther out from the surfaces seen by the naked eye that is only focused upon and identified with the overt presentations, outer forms and external appearances of phenomena.

True human beings are human beings of Spirit, Tao, Virtuosity/Te and Soul who are embodying, personifying, enacting and identifying *as* Tao and its dynamic-kinetic energetic operations that are the reality, ground, center and agency of the true attending relationship/process. True attenders are True human beings who are One with Heaven-Earth, the Universe, Nature and Humanity.

Appendix Two

The following are succinct statements for each one of the *Nei P'ien* tales that provide a quick reference to the essential message transmitted in each tale and/or its psychotherapeutic commentary.

RECORD ONE / *Carefree Wandering in Vastness*
1. Limited ego-mind can only wonder at the transcendent journey.
2. Theories and techniques are insufficient for the vast journey.
3. Transcendent flights require jettisoning excess baggage.
4. Self-regulating is the natural foundation for journeying.
5. Non-ordinary states and the transforming power of presence are real.
6. Relevant and useful ways of being facilitate Spiritual development.
7. Limited ego-mind cannot imagine transpersonal usefulness.
8. Tao is the most useful context and ground for Spiritual journeying.

RECORD TWO / *Equalizing Matters Discoursing*
1. Attuning to vital Ch'i energy supports the efficacy of Virtuosity.
2. Great understanding is compassionate regarding the human condition.
3. Tao-Self is the true regulator of human experience. Let it be.
4. Disidentifying from bodily states is vital for being and living.
5. Being true to Self and letting-be are identifying *as* Tao-nature.
6. Virtuosity is beyond absolute and fixed dualistic discriminations.

7. Tao's Clear Light illuminates the interchangeability of concepts.
8. What is acceptable is uniquely defined. Follow the natural course.
9. The One Reality of Tao unifies and harmonizes any and all differences.
10. Evaluative judgments are far downstream from Tao and No-Thingness.
11. The Mysterious Origin of human being cannot be known by the ego-mind.
12. Let paradoxical unities be without proliferating dualities.
13. Accept experience without discriminating, debating or judging.
14. Not objectify and name the many realities of human experiencing.
15. In Tao's Clear Inner Light, non-knowing is perfect understanding.
16. Be humbly awed by the profound magnitude of our Virtuosity.
17. Understand the impossibility of absolutely knowing distinctions.
18. Awaken from the dream-filled slumber of our ordinary lives.
19. Harmonize good-bad and right-wrong in the Heavenly Equality of Tao.
20. Cease expecting that changing shadows can create constant light.
21. Consider that our reality may be some other being's dream.

RECORD THREE / *Nourishing Life's Host*
1. Live at the central pivotal axis and middle way of Tao to conserve energy.
2. Intuitively following the energy of Spirit is nourishing life.
3. Being ourselves preserves Heaven-given Spirit and Virtuosity.

4. Spirit continues to live on while we human beings come and go.

RECORD FOUR / *Being Human amid Worldly Affairs*
1. Well-meaning assisting requires self-development to complete it.
2. The goodness and kindness of Virtuosity is compromised by ego-needs.
3. True assisting involves Virtuosity and not plans and strategies.
4. Heart-mind fasting empties ego and opens to the energy of Spirit.
5. True Virtuosity is being devoted and loyal to our Heart-of-Hearts.
6. Truthfulness begets trust and going along fosters completion.
7. Successful assisting involves understanding and following unique natures.
8. Being relatively 'useless' is useful for extending life.
9. Being relatively 'useless' preserves the integrity of Spirit.
10. Virtuosity is incredibly resilient in preserving Spirit and life.
11. Drop the heavy boulder of sadness and lift the light feather of happiness.

RECORD FIVE / *Virtuosity Fulfilling Agreement*
1. True Virtuosity is the power of presence and not the presence of power.
2. True Virtuosity transcends external and physical forms and status.
3. Unfortunate experiences are springboards for Spiritual growth.
4. Nourishing life preserves the integrity of Spirit and Virtuosity.
5. Wholehearted Virtuosity is fully harmonizing with transformings.

6. Formless Virtuosity is perfectly balancing to an openness.
7. Virtuosity's radiant luminosity shines forth in appearances.
8. Being nourished by Nondual Tao completes Virtuosity/Tao-nature.
9. Not waste Virtuosity and precious Human Being by overanalyzing things.

RECORD SIX / *Great Kindred Teacher*
1. True human beings accord with their Heavenly Tao-nature.
2. True human beings do not use ego-mind to assist Heaven.
3. True human beings are impartial, compassionate and beneficial.
4. True human beings are grounded, centered and spacious beings.
5. True human beings live and die for the Reality of Heavenly Tao.
6. True human beings live and die to the actualities of Earthly Tao.
7. True human beings identify *as* Tao and enjoy its endless changes.
8. True human beings affirm and transcend everything *as* Tao.
9. True human beings let things be and go along with things *as* they are.
10. True human beings step back and obey Tao's transformings and workings.
11. True human beings are nourished by, thrive in and are 'lost' in Tao.
12. True human beings have awakened from the ego-dream of being an 'I'.
13. True human beings have forgotten externals and wander with Tao.
14. True human beings have forgotten every 'thing' and identify *as* Tao.

15. True human beings accept the mysterious workings of Tao.

RECORD SEVEN / *Appropriate Attending and Regulating*
1. True leaders are clear, empty, still and question answers.
2. True leaders are clear, empty, still and act appropriately.
3. True leaders are pure, simple, allowing and following along.
4. True sages are naturally harmonizing, transforming and completing.
5. True masters are able to control and utilize vital Ch'i energies.
6. True masters are not lost in abstractions and wander in vastness.
7. True masters preserve the wholeness of Primordial Tao.

The following are succinct statements for each of the *Nei P'ien* tales cited in Appendix One of this rendition that similarly provide a quick reference to the essential message transmitted in each tale and/or its psychotherapeutic commentary.

1. THE CICADA CATCHER – the value of steadiness and one-pointedness.
2. THE FERRYMAN – the value of forgetting context, medium and process.
3. THE ARCHER – the value of not externalizing, competing or 'trying'.
4. THE ROOSTER TRAINER – the value of constancy, focus and stillness.
5. THE SWIMMER – the value of going with, following and unself-consciousness.
6. THE BELL STAND CARVER – the value of forgetting, emptiness and matching.
7. FORGETTING – the value of allowing, changing, comfort and forgetting.
8. NOURISHING A BIRD – the value of Nature-appropriate

nourishing.
9. THE EMPTY BOAT – the value of vacancy, emptiness and openness.
10. THE BELL MAKER – the value of oneness, simplicity and letting-be.
11. THE BUCKLE MAKER – the value of single-mindedness and whole-heartedness.
12. DOG AND HORSE JUDGING – the value of being egoless and unself-conscious.
13. FORGETTING WORDS – the value of getting meanings and forgetting words.
14. DOUBLE INJURY – the value of not forcing the overcoming of inclinations.
15. CHUANG TZU'S FUNERAL – the value of impartiality, truth and fairness.

Appendix Three

The following are abridged and paraphrased excerpts from the Outer and Miscellaneous Chapters of Burton Watson's translation of *The Complete Works of Chuang Tzu*. They are sequentially listed by chapter and page number.

The Outer Chapters

8–103 Expertness means following the true form of inborn nature.
9–105 In uncarved simplicity, we attain our true nature.
10–113 Great confusion comes from coveting knowledge.
11–122 Rest in inaction and beings will transform of themselves.
12–128 Without Tao, the body has no life. Without Virtuosity, life has no clarity.
13–143 Emptiness, stillness, limpidity, silence and inaction are the root of all beings.
14–166 Getting hold of Tao, there is nothing that cannot be done.
15–168 The lives of True human beings are the working of Heaven.
16–171 Tao is order. Virtuosity is harmony.
17–182 Heaven is on the inside. Human Being is on the outside.
18–191 The inaction of Heaven-Earth and Human Being is purity, peace and happiness.
19–197 Forgetting the world and life, vitality is whole and one with Heaven.
20–210 Only Tao and Virtuosity can be relied upon.
21–225 True human beings attain complete Beauty and wander in complete Happiness.

22–234   Rest in Tao without cognition, practices and procedures.

The Miscellaneous Chapters

23–259   Tao is Virtuosity's model. Life is Virtuosity's light.
24–276   True human beings embrace Tao and follow along with the world.
25–281   True human beings approach everything in a Spirit of unity and effortlessness.
26–300   True human beings wander in the world without taking sides.
27–304   True human beings harmonize everything with Heavenly Equality.
28–317   Forget forms, bodies and minds and arrive at Tao.
29–330   Time lost in anxiety, worry and illness leaves 4-5 days a month for laughing.
30–342   The sword of Heaven is brought forth in accord with Yin/Yang.
31–349   The Spirit of the Inner Truth of Tao moves external beings.
32–356   True human beings embody Great Origin, Unity, Purity and Tranquility.
33–362   The 'Art of Tao' is making Heaven, source; Virtuosity, root; Tao, gate and Transformation, Self.

NOTES

1. Definitions of the Chinese characters appearing throughout this rendition are integrating etymological radicals and phonetics and philosophical extended meanings.

2. Kuan Yin Hsi is the purported Guardian of the Pass who requests that Lao Tzu share his wisdom before leaving China which he records and which becomes known as the *Book of Lao Tzu* or *Tao Te Ching*. See the companion book *Lao Tzu's Tao Te Ching. Psychotherapeutic Commentaries. A Wayfaring Counselor's Rendering of the Tao Virtuosity Experience.*

3. The usual translations of Te are 'virtue' and 'power'. In this rendition, Te is translated as 'Virtuosity' and considered as:
    1. The absolutely unique individualizing of Tao.
    2. Our innermost / deepest / centermost / truest / utmost Tao-nature.
    3. The efficacious power of Tao to in-fluence (create in-flowing).
    4. Our inborn/innate gifts/talents/genius.
    5. Our inner truth/integrity straightforwardly expressed.
    6. Our intrinsic/inherent Heart-of-Hearts.

4. Although Yin/Yang is only explicitly referred to twice in both Interior Records 4 and 6, over eighty-five bipolar complements appear throughout the seven *Interior Records*, e.g.,

Heaven-Earth	Light-shadow	True-false
Absolute-relative	Great-small	Right-wrong
Nonbeing-being	Long-short lived	Good-bad
Mystery-destiny	Broad-narrow	Success-failure
Unlimited-limited	Free-bound	Gain-loss
Constant-changing	Mind-body	Merit-dishonor
Complete-incomplete	Awake-dreaming	Acceptable-unacceptable
Unity-multiplicity	Life-death	Likes-dislike
	Useless-useful	This-that

5. Ch'i, the vital energy and life force of Tao, is both cosmic/nonmaterial and ontic/material and is considered to be identical to the transcendence and immanence of Tao.

6. Passages of the Human Spirit and Soul are explicitly treated in the companion book entitled *Lao Tzu's Tao Te Ching. Soul Journeying Commentaries. A Sojourning Pilgrim's Rendering of 81 Spirit Soul Passages.*

7. During the microlab basic counseling skills training of psychology graduate students, fully attending and clearly listening are found to create experiences of safe contact and deep connection that open the way to rapport, self-disclosure, genuine communication, self-awareness, insight and expression without the necessity of utilizing other facilitative skills.

8. In the commentaries of this rendition, and in keeping with the etymological definition of psychotherapy as 'attending the Soul', the word 'attending' is used for the psychotherapy/counseling relationship/process. Psychotherpists/counselors are referred to as 'true attenders' and patients/counselees are referred to as 'human beings' and/or 'human beings engaged in the attending relationship/process'.

The various grammatical forms of the word 'attending' also relate to four of the main experiential concepts of Te, Yin/Yang Ch'i, Wu Wei Ch'i and Tao in the following ways:

TE	– being *attentive* to needs/mindful/heedful.
	– paying *attention* to details/observing/focusing.
YIN/YANG CH'I	– *attendant* factors/concomitant circumstances/connected consequences.
WU WEI CH'I	– *attending* to business/applied looking after.
	– being an *attendant*/performing a service.
TAO	– an *attending* therapist/caregiving/overseeing.
	– an *attender*/present at/participating in.

True attenders are present for, mindful of, interrelated with, attentive to, watching over, looking after and caring for the human beings with whom they are engaged and involved.

9. Possibly, the same Lieh Tzu who is characterized in *The Lieh Tzu*, an ancient Taoist text, and who is considered to be one of the 'originators' of Chinese Taoism, along with Lao Tzu and Chuang Tzu.

10. Hui Shih Tzu (c. 370-310 BCE), is a philosopher/logician who is concerned with logical paradoxes, the relationship of names to reality, the relativity of space and time, and the unifying of opposites and who is often cast as a 'straight man' enabling Chuang Tzu to illustrate his own contrasting viewpoints.

11. In a footnote, Watson writes that 'Heaven is not something different from earth and man, but a name applied to the natural and spontaneous functioning of the two'. (Watson pp. 37).

12. The question is much more relevant today but also much more difficult to unequivocally answer given the extent of social networking 'tweeting' and 'twittering'.

13. So as not to 'confuse us' (pun intended), Chuang Tzu often has Confucius speaking the words of a Taoist sage as a way of portraying him as allied with the natural Tao of Taoism rather than with the Confucian 'Tao' as the 'correct' way of the moral codes, rules, rites, roles and social ethics of benevolence/Jen, righteousness/I and propriety/Li of the ideal princely gentleman/Chun Tzu.

14. Great liberty is taken in identifying these various characterizations of True Human Beings. Interpretations of this section differ widely among translations and the entire section may be a later Legalist interpolation (Watson pp. 79), since many of the described qualities appear to be incongruous with Chuang Tzu's personifications of True Human Beings.

15. These progressive stages can be used as meditative guidelines for self-cultivating and returning to Tao. A similar progressive journeying is depicted and described in the Zen Buddhist ox-herding pictures, where the ox metaphorically symbolizes the original state of awakened/illuminated/enlightened consciousness as follows;

1. Seeking the lost ox longingly/a vague sense of Tao.
2. Finding ox-tracks scripturally/a clear concept of Tao.
3. Glimpsing the whole ox fleetingly/a fleeting glimpse of Tao.
4. Encountering the wild ox directly/a direct experiencing of Tao.
5. Taming the ox steadfastly/internalizing of Tao.
6. Riding the ox home joyfully/identifying *as* Tao.
7. Forgetting the ox completely/forgetting Tao.
8. Forgetting the self peacefully/forgetting Tao-Self.
9. Returning to the Origin openly/returning to Original Tao.
10. Entering the marketplace radiantly/being Tao in the world.

16. Translations of the title of Record Seven made in the references cited in this rendition of the *Nei P'ien* are 'Fit for Emperors and Kings' (Watson), 'The Sage-King' (Feng and English) and 'Responsive Leadership' (Cleary).

A literal translation of the three characters of the title reads something like 'Proper/Suitable/Necessary for Emperors/Sovereigns/Rulers and Kings/Princes/Rulers.' Many of the tales involve questions, advice and guidelines regarding governing and the characteristics, qualities and activities of rulers.

In keeping with the focus of this rendition on 'attending', Record Seven is titled 'Appropriate Attending and Regulating' to emphasize the fittingness, harmonizing, guiding, serving and liberating attending and regulating behaviors of rulers and leaders rather than their being correct, controlling, forceful, directing, dominating and restricting.

True attending is the numinous awakening to the constant co-presencing of authentic egoless being, communing and uniting in relationships and True regulating is the harmonious balancing of the continuous co-creating of rhythmic seamless unfolding, flowing and proceeding in processes.

True attending and True regulating are the quintessentially appropriate responsiveness of both emperors/kings ruling/governing empires/kingdoms and of psychotherapists/counselors conducting/guiding the attending relationship/process of psychotherapy/counseling.

Such True attending and True regulating naturally constitute the illuminating, harmonizing, healing and transformative power of the spontaneous Presence/Tzu Jan and inner Tao-nature/Virtuosity/Te of True human beings/Chen Jen who are uniquely individualizing, embodying, assimilating, personifying, enacting and consciously identifying *as* Tao and the operating of its dynamic Yin/Yang Ch'i and kinetic Wu Wei Ch'i vital energies.

True attenders are self-aware, self-monitoring, self-regulating, self-transforming and self-developing and are purely, simply, openly and fully accepting of, according with, allowing of and abiding in the natural processes and organic rhythms of human being, existing, living and experiencing in the attending relationship process.

17. It is not suggested or advised that the uninitiated can or should attempt to control, direct, manipulate or interfere with the natural alternating and flowing Yin/Yang Ch'i and Wu Wei Ch'i vital energies that reside, balance, circulate and transmute in the lower/ belly, middle/ heart and upper/head energy centers/elixir fields/Tan T'iens and microcosmic/macrocosmic orbits of the human body.

The following schema delineates these centers, energies and activities:

Belly Center/ Lower Tan T'ien	Heart Center/ Middle Tan T'ien	Head Center/ Upper Tan T'ien
Vitality/Ching	Energy/Ch'i	Spirit/Shen
Earth Energy/ Yin Ch'i	Human Energy/ Yin/Yang Ch'i	Heaven Energy/ Yang Ch'i
Generating/ Originating	Circulating/ Harmonizing	Transmuting/ Illuminating
Reserved/Contained	Conserved/Maintained	Preserved/Sustained
Stilling Will	Emptying Heart	Clearing Mind

Ways of conserving, nourishing, cultivating, compounding and circulating vital Ch'i energies can be learned and practiced through closely supervised mentoring by Tao-Masters, as can yogic ways of alchemically transmuting generative energy/Ching to vital energy/Ch'i to Spiritual energy/Shen within, between and throughout the energy fields, centers and orbits of the human body.

Beyond the three elixir fields and energy centers in the human body is the undifferentiated and formless state of Non-Beingness, emptiness and openness before the originating, forming, manifesting and completing of beings and things. This is the Plenum Void/Wu Chi of pre-differentiated Primordial Ch'i energy or of perfectly balanced Yin Ch'i/Yang Ch'i vital energies that is a neutral/zero/void state at its maximum potential for manifesting forms, things and beings. It is the actualizing of this awesome potentiality that frightened the Shaman of Record 7-5 and is the undifferentiated pristine reality of Hun Tun that was destroyed in Record 7-7.

18. So, in good Taoist fashion, the seven *Interior Records* come full circle from beginning to ending.

The first Record is beginning with a Great Yang bird/P'eng, the legendary Roc of the Southern Darkness; regularly migrating, alternating and transforming into a Great Yin fish/K'un, the fabulous Leviathan of the Northern Darkness, in the vast and spacious reality of a boundless, limitless, transcendent and encompassing realm beyond the ordinary experiencing of human beings.

The last Record is ending with a Southern Sea Yang ruler/Shu regularly converging, meeting and transacting with a Northern Sea Yin ruler/Hu in the small and specious actuality of a bounded, limited, immanent and centralized world within the ordinary experiencing of human beings.

The following organizes these relationships:

PSYCHOTHERAPEUTIC COMMENTARIES / 245

RECORD ONE	**RECORD SEVEN**
Natural activity	Unnatural actions
Cyclical/regular	Linear/irregular
Maintains wholeness	Violates integrity
Shares space	Controls center
Embodies equality	Forces sameness
Preserves alternating	Invades wholeness
Transforms/recreates	Deforms/destroys

The following characterizes the Yin/Yang relationships in Records 1 and 7:

YIN	**YANG**
Northern Darkness	Southern Darkness
Earthly/water realm	Heavenly/air realm
K'un/Great Fish/Leviathan	P'eng/Great Bird/Roc
Northern Sea Ruler	Southern Sea Ruler
Hu/sudden/unexpected	Shu/sudden abrupt
Hasty/careless	Hasty/brief
Homophones =	Homophones =
Reckless/foolish	Quick/careless
Dark/obscure	Light/bright

YIN/YANG
CENTRAL REGION

HUN	**TUN**
Turbid/chaotic	Turbid/chaotic
Undifferentiated/mixed	Undifferetiated/mixed
Blended/confused	Blended/confused
Homophones =	Homophones =
Mixed/confused	Sudden/immediate
Muddled/stupid	Dull/blunt
Dark/dull	Obtuse/hidden

In Record One, transcendent Yin/Yang Beings embody and reflect, with awesome magnificence, the vastness and greatness of Tao by freely, naturally and regularly transforming Tao as their own Reality. In Record Seven, immanent yin/yang rulers violate and destroy, with gruesome beneficence, the centeredness and wholeness of Tao by carelessly, unnaturally and irregularly converting Tao in their own image. Such is the enormous difference between instinctually and intuitively concretizing, internalizing, assimilating and Self-identifying *as* Tao, Spirit, Being and Soul and conceptually and projectively abstracting, externalizing, objectifying and ego-identifying with 'others', 'objects', 'things' and 'doings'.

In the seamless Great Cycling of human be-ing and living, endings are new beginnings and deaths are re-births and new lives. Each and every one of us precious transient human beings is concluding, completing, consummating, culminating and fulfilling and is re-creating, re-birthing, re-turning and re-newing the wholeness of Constant Eternal Tao, whether we know it or not.

19. In Records 27 and 33 of *The Chuang Tzu* text, reference is made to Chuang Tzu's descriptions of three different kinds of words:

1. Yu Yen/lodged/residing/spoken words that are allegorical, figurative, metaphorical and illustrative; are imputed, ascribed and attributed to others, outsiders, historical and fictional figures and are used to give compelling depth, breadth and credence to expositions. These words are the abstract, indirect and mediating jargon of philosophers, psychologists and theoreticians that comprise 90% of ordinary once-removed talk.

2. Chung/Ch'ung Yen/double/repeated/spoken words that are weighty, multi-layered, lofty, authoritative, wise and final; are made by historical venerables, elders and teachers and are used to give the ring of truth to, and bring an end to, discussions, polemic discourses and debates. These words are the abstract, indirect and mediating rhetoric of master psychotherapists/

counselors and founders of 'schools' of psychotherapy/counseling that comprise 70% of twice told double talk.

3. CHIH YEN/goblet/measuring cup/funnel shaped words that follow along with natural courses; continually pour out endless changes; harmonize matters in Heavenly Unity and Equality and lead to No-Words that speak nothing but say everything. These are the concrete, direct, immediate and salvific words that, like a goblet, tip when full, spill over, pour out and right when empty. 'Wow' 'far out', 'right on', 'great', 'awesome', 'amazing', 'astonishing', 'miraculous', 'marvelous', 'magnificent', 'wonderful', 'splendid', 'perfect', 'exactly', 'beautiful', 'precious', 'yes', 'That's It!'

Epilogue

In psychotherapy/counseling, many of the questions to answer are grounded in the beclouded ill-knowings of mental ignorance. Many of the conflicts to resolve are centered in the overfilled ill-havings of emotional attachment. Many of the problems to solve are originated by the too busy ill-doings of volitional error. And many of the alienations to repair are experienced in the often strange ill-beings of relational separation. Abstaining from mental clutter and relinquishing emotional filler open the way to sourcing volitional actions and uniting relational interactions in/*as* Tao.

The Way of Ignoring

Ignoring is a knowing *about* things/beings and not letting them be *as*/what/who they are. By thinking, ideating, imagining and symbolizing; what is embodied, uniquely individualized, constituted and empowered (Te) is abstracted, conceived, construed, defined, named, classified and categorized *into* mental object-'contents'.

Because of mentally objectifying limitations such as sensing, perceiving, cognizing, concluding and the inferring of 'thing-contents' by the ego-mind; we are unable to let things/beings be; to simply witness and behold; to accept, acknowledge and appreciate; to authentically receive (not reject), empower, individualize and experience and to insightfully 'know', comprehend and partake of the Truth of Absolute/Mysterious Tao. What is True is epistemologically and logically unconceivable by the ignoring and clouded 'knowing' and reasonings of the phenomenal ego-mind.

The Tao of Abstaining

Ignoring is avoided and enlightened through the meditative practice of Heart-Mind Fasting (Letting-Be). A mental clearing occurs that is an awakening awareness, with Sharpest Mind, of consistently illuminating, noetically revealing (Te) and intuitively 'knowing' of the inborn nature of things, beings and ourselves *as* unique instantiations, embodiments and personifications of the Truth, Integrity, Wisdom and Light of Absolute Tao. And everything and everyone, so re-cognized and real-ized, are an absolutely and uniquely individualizing and consistently forming of this Absolute Tao.

The Way of Attaching

Attaching is a having *of* things/beings and not letting go of them or not letting them go. By wanting, seeking, getting and keeping; what is bipolar, dynamically alternating, centering and voiding (Yin/Yang Ch'i) is fixated into static one-sided, antithetical, mutually exclusive dualistic opposites, evaluated, judged, desired, pursued, acquired and possessed *into* emotional object-'goods'.

Because of emotionally objectifying attachments such as attraction, assessing, coveting, preferring and investing in 'thing-goods' by the ego-heart; we are unable to let things/beings go; to naturally encounter and release; to attune, adjust and accord; to accurately reflect (not retain), equalize, interrelate and equilibrate and to inherently 'have', coincide with and mirror the Good of Essential/Miraculous Tao. What is Good is aesthetically and axiologically unattainable by the attaching and filling 'having' and ownings of the phenomenal ego-heart.

The Tao of Relinquishing

Attachments are withdrawn and divested through the meditative practice of Sitting Forgetting (Letting-Go). An emotional emptying occurs that is an accomodating transiency, with Deepest Heart, of continually manifesting, dynamically alternating (Yin/Yang Ch'i) and complementarily 'having' of the inner core of things, beings and ourselves *as* perfect correspondences with, interchangings and reflections of the Good, Beauty, Harmony and Love of Essential Tao. And everything and everyone, so embraced and centered, are an essentially and equally interrelating and continually transforming of this Essential Tao.

The Way of Error

Erring is a doing *to* things/beings and not going-with them *as*/how they are going. By fabricating motives, goals, plans and strategies; what is originating, kinetically flowing, seamless and unfolding (Wu Wei Ch'i) is interfered with, intervened upon, managed, controlled, manipulated, forced and directed *into* volitional object-'deeds'.

Because of volitionally objectifying intendings such as devising, contriving, initiating, implementing and the executing of 'thing-deeds' by the ego-will; we are unable to go-with things/beings; to spontaneously yield and follow; to accede, allow and accompany; to appropriately respond (not react), enact, actualize and proceed and to instinctually 'do', assent and conform to the Right of Ultimate/Marvelous Tao. What is Right is ethically and politically unachievable by the erroneous and busy 'doing' and purposings of the phenomenal ego-will.

The Tao of Sourcing

Error is prevented and eliminated through the meditative practice of Origin Wandering (Going-With). A volitional stilling occurs that is an agreeing complying, with Highest Will, of continuously sourcing, kinetically unfolding (Wu Wei Ch'i) and effortless 'doing' from the indwelling fountainhead of things, beings and ourselves as original creations, enactments and activities of the Right, Grace, Peace and Law of Ultimate Tao. And everything and everyone, so originated and actualized, are an ultimately and originally creating and continuously enacting of this Ultimate Tao.

The Way of Separating

Separating is being *apart* or *away from* things/beings and not being-with them *as*/what/who they are being. By relating to things/beings as 'out there', 'over there', 'hers', 'hims', 'thems', 'its' and 'those'; what is interbeing, ontologically associated, joined, interconnected, integrated, whole and complete (Tao) is distanced, isolated, alienated, fragmented, excluded and dissociated *into* relational object-'others'.

Because of relationally objectifying separations such as marginalizing, infantalizing, stigmatizing, pathologizing and the invalidating of 'thing-others' by the ego-self; we are unable to be-with things/beings; to freely join and connect; to affiliate, ally and abide with; to availably return to (not restrict), engage, identify with and inSpirit and to intrinsically 'be', unite with and complete the Reality of One/Magnificent Tao. What is Real is metaphysically and ontologically unrealizable in the separate and strange 'being' and existings of the phenomenal ego-self.

The Tao of Uniting

Separations are integrated and healed through the meditative practice of Tao Residing (Being-With). A relational freeing occurs that is a uniting co-existing, with Greatest Spirit, of constantly pervading, ontically consummating (Tao) and essential 'being' at the innermost root of things, beings and ourselves as complete unions, identifications and identities *as* the Reality, Unity, Freedom and Life of One Tao. And everything and everyone, so animated and vitalized, are an entirely and integrally uniting and constantly completing of this One Tao.

The Way of Ego-Being

The way of human being, when exclusively and completely ego-identified, characterizes people as asleep and lost in clouded mental ignorance, filled emotional attachments, busy volitional errors and alienated relational separations. They are often living untrue, inauthentic and unwise lives; dualistic, oppositional and conflicted lives; controlling, pressured and coercing lives and divided, fragmented and estranged lives.

Such people are often egocentrically striving to be above, ahead and beyond; rather than humbly enjoying being below, behind and within; fellow human beings; and are often absorbed and preoccupied with the object-oriented knowing, having and doing of 'things' and the being of 'others'. They are often disinterested in, unwilling to or unable to acknowledge, accept and appreciate; align with, attune to and accord with; yield to, allow and follow; and join, connect and abide with the simple realities of ordinary human being and everyday human living.

Such egocentrically identified people often find the letting-be and letting-go of, and going-with and being-with, fellow human beings and the ordinariness of everydayness to be irrelevant, useless, difficult and even dangerous. They have not yet awakened from, and are not yet liberated from, the slumber of an ego-identifying dream that is displacing, eclipsing and obscuring the Reality, Truth, Freedom, Harmony and Peace of their Human Spirit and the Actuality, Wisdom, Beauty, Grace and Joys of their Human Soul.

Ego-identifying people are imprisoned in and shackled by limiting conceptual, emotional, volitional and relational confines and constraints that prevent them from experiencing the Truth of Higher Mind, the Goodness of Deeper Heart, the Rightness of Divine Will and the Reality of Ultimate Being. The Light of Tao is lost in the disfigured shadows of their darkness. The Love of Tao is lost in the heartless judgments of their coldness. The Law of Tao is lost in the accelerating velocity of their busyness. And the Life of Tao is lost in the barren wastelands of their aloneness.

The Tao of Tao Jen

Tao Jen, the Human Beings of/*as* Tao, the Sheng Jens/ Sacred/Wise Human Beings of Lao Tzu and the Chen Jens/ True/Free Human Beings of Chuang Tzu, are ego-free of the mental ignorings, emotional attachings, volitional errings and relational separatings that cloud, fill, busy and estrange human beings from the letting-be, letting-go, going-with and being-with of just-what-*is*-so just-*as*-it-is-so.

Tao Jen are awakened, transformed, integrated, perfected, and liberated Human Beings. They are being, living and experiencing a clearness of Mind, emptiness of Heart, stillness of Will, oneness of Being and freeness of Spirit, an openness that is the Ground of Truth, Integrity and Wisdom; the Center of Good, Beauty and Harmony; the Flow of Right, Grace and Peace and the Spaciousness of Reality, Unity and Freedom.

The culminating experiencing of Absolute, Essential, Ultimate and One Tao occurs *as* the True Mind, Good Heart, Right Will, Real Being and Free Spirit of Tao Jen; the Sacred and wise, true and free Human Beings who are Tao-bestowed and endowed (en-Tao-ed), Tao-focused and centered, Tao-embodied and personified, Tao-realized and actualized, Tao-returned and identified and Tao-like. They are *Being*-Tao; the Light, Love, Law and Life that *is* Tao; both *as* its Transcendent, Noumenal, Essential and Ultimate Reality, Absolute Unity and Identity *and as* its immanent, phenomenal, existential and intimate actualities, relative diversities and totality of the '10,000 things'/Wan Wu that are spontaneously presencing/Tzu Jan in their awakened consciousness, awareness and experiencing.

And some Tao Jen are human beings, so-called psychotherapists/counselors, who are wise and true attenders unequivocally called to, completely committed to, openly available for, fully engaged in and jointly participating in, the professional practice of the attending relationship/process of psychotherapy/counseling; and who are beneficially encouraging, supporting, assisting, facilitating and guiding the awakening, healing, transforming, developing and well-being of fellow human beings, so-called patients/counselees.

TAO

Road/way/path
Speak/lead/guide
Principle/doctrine
Reality/Logos/Truth
Law/order/method
The Way

T'UNG

Together/with
United/union/reunion
Share in/agreement
Alike/similar
Same as/identical
As

The reality of Tao exists *as* the awakened and illuminated Consciousness of human beings who have concluded, completed, consummated and culminated the experience of human being by embodying, assimilating, enacting, personifying and fully identifying *as* Tao. They are the Sacred/wise/Sheng Jen of Lao Tzu's *Tao Te Ching* and the true/free/Chen Jen of Chuang Tzu's *Nei P'ien*.

Such human beings/Tao Jen are Tao-focused and centered, Tao-realized and actualized, Tao-returned and identified, Tao-like and Being-Tao. They are being and living *as* the realities and actualities of Te/Virtuosity, the dynamics and kinetics of Yin/Yang Ch'i and Wu Wei Ch'i energies and the spontaneous presencing/Tzu Jan of all beings/things/Wan Wu.

These Tao Jen are purely and simply human beings sheerly and utterly just who/*as* they are being and are a most precious and treasured blessing, gift, opportunity and joy to be with and to experience whenever, wherever and however we can . . .

Coda

Chuang Tzu's *Interior Records/Nei P'ien* is the second volume of a *Taoist Trilogy* that includes Lao Tzu's *Tao Virtuosity Experience/Tao Te Ching* and Lieh Tzu's *Nature of Real Living/Hsing Shih Sheng*. The tales and commentaries of the *Interior Records/Nei P'ien* portray the nature, qualities, attributes, activities and relationships of True Human Beings/Chen Jen and of true attenders who are conducting the attending relationship/process of psychotherapy/counseling; both of whom are embodying, personifying, enacting and modeling a Tao-identified human being and living that is awakened, true, transformative, free and happy.

Identifying with the Spirit, Heart and Soul of Chuang Tzu and with True Human Beings/Chen Jen and true attenders, as characterized in the tales and commentaries of the *Interior Records/Nei P'ien*; opens the Way to ourselves being true human beings and true attenders who are attentively relating to human beings and who are being attentively related to by them. The Way is opened to being our own true Selves and to truly living our own lives in heartfelt, wholehearted and heartwarming ways that are more awake, conscious, authentic, liberated, spontaneous, intimate, fulfilling and enjoyable and that uniquely and harmoniously integrate our Heavenly Spirit and our Earthly body *as* our Human Soul.

REFERENCES

Cleary, Thomas (Trans.). *The Taoist Classics: Vol. One.* Boston: Shambhala Publications, Inc. 1990.
Feng, Gia-Fu and English, Jane (Trans.). *Chuang Tsu: Inner Chapters.* New York: Vintage Books. 1974.
Translation Division. *Zhuang Zi. The Chinese-English Bilingual Series of Chinese Classics. Vol. 7.* Hunan, China: Hunan Publishing House. 1996.
Watson, Burton (Trans.). *The Complete Works of Chuang Tzu.* New York: Columbia University Press. 1968.

All information concerning Chinese language and characters and Taoist history and terms is obtained from the following reference resources:

Dainian, Zhang. *Key Concepts in Chinese Philosophy.* Edmund Ryden (Ed. & Trans.). New Haven: Yale University Press/Beijing Foreign Languages Press. 2002.
Dong, Li. *Concise Chinese Dictionary: Chinese-English/English-Chinese.* Rutland, Vermont: Tuttle Publishing. 2015.
Fenn, C.H.. *The Five Thousand Dictionary: Chinese-English.* Cambridge: Harvard University Press. 1976.
Fischer-Schreiber, Ingrid. *The Shambhala Dictionary of Taoism.* Werner Wunsche (Trans.). Boston: Shambhala Publications, Inc.. 1996.
Huang, Quanyu; Chen, Tong and Huang, Kuangyan. *McGraw-Hill's Chinese Dictionary & Guide to 20,000 Essential Words.* New York: McGraw Hill. 2010.
Kluemper, Michael L. and Nadeau, Kit-Yee Yam. *Mandarin Chinese Characters Made Easy.* Rutland, Vermont: Tuttle Publishing. 2016.

Kohn, Livia. *Zhuangzi: Text and Context.* Honolulu: Three Pines Press. 2014.

Matthews, Alison and Matthews, Laurence. *Learning Chinese Characters.* Rutland, Vermont: Tuttle Publishing. 2007.

Matthews, R.H. *Matthew's Chinese-English Dictionary* Cambridge: Harvard University Press. 1943.

McNaughton, William and Ying, Lee. *Reading and Writing Chinese: Traditional Character Edition.* Rutland, Vermont: Tuttle Publishing. 1999.

Wieger, L.. *Chinese Characters: Their Origin, Etymology, History, Classification and Signification.* L. Davrout (Trans.). New York: Dover Publications, Inc.. 1966.

Wilder, G.D. and Ingram, J.H. *Analysis of Chinese Characters.* New York: Dover Publications, Inc.. 1974.

Wong, Eva. *Taoism: An Essential Guide.* Boston: Shambhala Publications, Inc.. 1997.

Wong, Eva. *Being Taoist: Wisdom for Living a Balanced Life.* Boston: Shambhala Publications, Inc.. 2015.

All information concerning English language definitions is obtained from:

Webster's New Collegiate Dictionary. Springfield, Massachusetts: G. & C. Merriam Co.. 1979.

About the Author

Ray Vespe received his B.A. Psychology degree from Cornell University (1958), M.S. Clinical Psychology degree from Case Western Reserve University (1959) and Ph.D. Counseling Psychology degree from the California Institute of Integral Studies (1986). He has educated, trained, supervised, counseled and mentored graduate students in the Integral Counseling Psychology program at CIIS (1972-1990), the Transpersonal Psychology program at the California Institute of Transpersonal Psychology (1977-1979) and the Transpersonal Counseling Psychology program at John F. Kennedy University (1978-1990). Ray has worked in a wide variety of inpatient, outpatient, agency and group treatment settings and was Clinical Director of the Integral Counseling Center (1975-1978/1982-1990), San Leandro Community Counseling (1990-1992) and Marin Treatment Center (1992-2004). He has been a student of Tao for sixty-two years, has engaged in psychotherapy work for fifty-seven years and has maintained a licensed private practice for forty-four of those years. Ray is currently retired and living in Sonoma County, California.

www.ingramcontent.com/pod-product-compliance
Lightning Source LLC
Chambersburg PA
CBHW070051080526
44586CB00013B/1005